MAKING
TQM WORK

Better Management Skills

This highly popular range of inexpensive paperbacks covers all areas of basic management. Practical, easy to read and instantly accessible, these guides will help managers to improve their business or communication skills. Those marked * are available on audio cassette.

The books in this series can be tailored to specific company requirements. For further details, please contact the publisher, Kogan Page, telephone 0171 278 0433, fax 0171 837 6348.

Be a Successful Supervisor
Business Etiquette
Coaching Your Employees
Conducting Effective Interviews
Creative Decision-making
Creative Thinking in Business
Counselling Your Staff
Delegating for Results
Effective Meeting Skills
Effective Performance Appraisals*
Effective Presentation Skills
Empowerment
First Time Supervisor
Get Organised!
Goals and Goal Setting
How to Communicate Effectively*
How to Develop a Positive
 Attitude*
How to Develop Assertiveness
How to Motivate People*
How to Understand Financial
 Statements
How to Write a Staff Manual
Improving Employee
 Performance
Improving Relations at Work
Keeping Customers for Life
Leadership Skills for Women

Learning to Lead
Make Every Minute Count*
Managing Disagreement
 Constructively
Managing Organisational
 Change
Managing Part-Time Employees
Managing Quality Customer
 Service
Managing Your Boss
Marketing for Success
Memory Skills in Business
Mentoring
Office Management
Productive Planning
Project Management
Quality Customer Service
Rate Your Skills as a Manager
Sales Training Basics
Self-Managing Teams
Selling Professionally
Speed Reading in Business
Successful Negotiation
Successful Telephone Techniques
Systematic Problem-solving and
 Decision-making
Team Building
Training Methods that Work

MAKING TQM WORK

Kit Sadgrove

KOGAN
PAGE

To Alexandra: a woman with zero defects

First published in 1995

Kogan Page Limited
120 Pentonville Road
London N1 9JN

British Library Cataloguing in Publication Data

A CIP record for this book is available from the British Library.

ISBN 0–7494–1521–5

Printed and bound in Great Britain by
Biddles Ltd, Guildford and King's Lynn

Contents

Note
Throughout the book I have used the word 'he' for the sake of simplicity. Women and men participate equally in TQM, which is the opposite of the macho kind of hire-and-fire management.

Acknowledgements
I am grateful to many people for their advice, especially Michael Ballard and Andrew Saunders. Any errors are mine alone.

CHAPTER 1
What is TQM?

In this chapter, you'll learn about:

- The four challenges facing organisations
- The need for continuous all-round improvement
- Why TQM is the right solution.

In the past manufacturers could sell all they made. Banks and restaurants didn't worry about the service they provided. Now things have changed. The four challenges shown in Figure 1.1 are forcing organisations to adapt.

Companies now have to be more responsive, offer a better product, and keep improving. In this book we see how you can achieve that through Total Quality Management (TQM).

How TQM works
TQM increases customer satisfaction by boosting quality. It does this by motivating the workforce and improving the way the company operates.

---

1. Customers are more demanding
The customer is more sophisticated and knowledgeable. If you don't offer good service, he will buy from a competitor. When corporate customers start improving their own quality, they

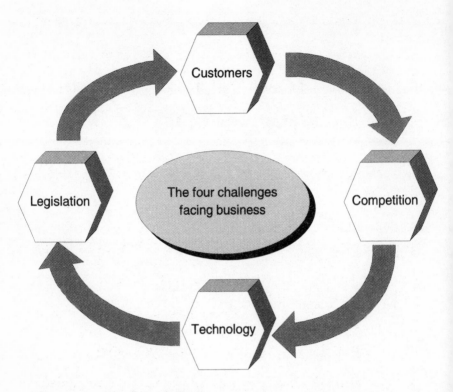

Figure 1.1 The four challenges

also expect better performance from their suppliers.

Corporate customers are also reducing the number of suppliers, which makes life even tougher.

2. Competition is greater

Competition is getting harder and becoming global. One buyer said, 'I'm just as likely to get a sales call from Malaysia as from Manchester.'

The fast-growing countries of East Asia often produce at low cost. This may be because of low wage costs or large investment. As a result, prices in many markets have fallen. Others will start to drop.

It is easy for a company to get caught between improved

Western products and low-price products from emerging countries.

Many companies now produce a new model in half the time it previously took. Some products have a much shorter life than before. At one time a building society wouldn't alter the style of its savings accounts for decades. Now it may add or delete accounts from one year to the next.

Change has even taken place in mature public-service organisations. Among hospitals, local government, railways and schools each institution is trying to get an advantage over the other.

3. Technology is changing

Even companies in traditional industries are finding that things are being done differently. Companies are using biotechnology, fibre optics, ultrasound and neural networks to make faster and better products.

New plastics, ceramics and adhesives are making ordinary products out of date. Service organisations are using information technology to respond faster and faster.

4. Legislation is making greater demands on companies

Environmental, health and safety laws now require companies to run safe and pollution-free businesses. No longer can you simply pour toxic liquids down the drain. Employees have to be careful to avoid environmental damage. This requires a motivated and knowledgeable workforce.

Yet companies have not woken up to these changes

Many companies are complacent. They're used to customers sending in orders. They are accustomed to supplying products which have faults in them. In today's competitive climate, they will start to lose customers. As one guru said, 'Survival is not obligatory.'

Some companies think they have no problems. This is especially true of monopoly suppliers and market leaders with popular products. Success makes companies complacent. Yet history proves that the most successful market leaders invariably fall the heaviest. IBM, which lost its grip on the computer market, is just one example.

Many companies are reluctant to change. They think that the systems that have made them successful will continue to work in the future. They feel uncomfortable making changes, or they lack the energy.

Inefficiency exists inside every company. Errors add cost, and reduce customer satisfaction. In the average firm, the cost of doing things wrong can be 25 per cent of turnover. Many staff spend a day a week rectifying problems (which is a 20 per cent failure rate). Doing things twice is a waste of time and effort. Many problems are never solved, and just recur.

How quality affects the customer

As a customer you are surrounded by examples of bad quality. It is not just that things are well made or badly made. It goes further than that. Here are some examples of quality failure:

- The kettle whose spout spills water
- The incomprehensible printer manual
- The letter from your children's school which contains spelling errors
- The café where the staff ignore their customers
- The brochure that takes weeks to arrive, or never actually comes.

Inside your own organisation, you can probably see other quality problems:

- The project which runs over time and over budget
- The R&D department whose members are always obstructive
- The products which are made wrongly, and have to be redone.

You need the four essentials

You know that your product and service could be improved. And you know that outside pressures are growing. So how do you respond?

You need to achieve the four essentials, which are shown in Figure 1.2. Often grouped under the word 'quality', they include the following techniques. You can:

- *Reduce defects*. This means reducing the number of errors made, whether in making products that don't work, or in making paperwork mistakes.

- *Improve productivity* (in other words, produce a greater output for the same level of cost).

- *Improve customer service*. Even companies in technical or capital intensive markets need to satisfy their customers.

- *Innovate*. Competitors are constantly offering your customer newer and better products. Yours have to match that rate of innovation.

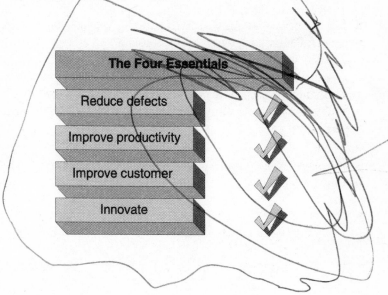

Figure 1.2 The four essentials

You can only achieve these four essentials if the energies of your whole workforce are committed to excellence and to the customer. The four essentials are too big a task for any one individual to achieve.

Defining the solution is simple, but achieving it is less easy. Companies and gurus have wrestled with the problem for years. Next we examine some of the ways it has been tackled.

Methods for improving quality

Various strategies have been tried. The early attempts used *statistical techniques* on the factory floor. In the 1960s, companies used *management by objectives* to try to control what happened. But managers sometimes forgot to motivate staff, so the results fell short of their target.

Incentive payment schemes (such as *piecework*) were brought in to boost productivity. But often this produced lots of poorly made products.

Then companies introduced *management systems*, such as ISO 9000. But staff sometimes ignored the new systems, and worked the way they always had.

The most recent fashions have been *benchmarking, partnership sourcing* and *business process re-engineering*. But these new tools often solve problems in only one area of the business, such as supplier quality or excellence in manufacturing.

So that leaves Total Quality Management, or TQM.

TQM is not as fashionable as re-engineering, nor as firmly defined as ISO 9000. But it contains all the elements for the successful company of the future.

Without TQM, you have to pray that your competitors remain incompetent. Use TQM properly, and your success is assured.

So what is TQM?

TQM is one of the vaguest business tools ever invented. There is no TQM bible, and each of the many quality gurus said something different. That makes it very confusing.

Everyone has their own view of how TQM should be applied.

But as the case histories in this book show, there is more than one route towards TQM. You adapt it to meet the needs of *your* business. Many elements are common, and those are the ones highlighted in this book.

TQM means satisfying customers first time, every time. It means enabling your employees to solve problems and eliminate waste. TQM is not so much a management technique as a whole style of working. TQM is really just another word for good management.

It is difficult, perhaps impossible, to achieve total quality. But companies that aim for it are going in the right direction.

Where it came from
Ignored for years in his own country, W Edwards Deming was a US statistician who held strong views on how to achieve excellence in manufacturing. Just after the Second World War, he was invited to Japan, where he talked about quality to packed audiences.

The Japanese quickly adopted his ideas, which contributed to Japan's miraculous post-war success. Later, the USA and other Western countries adopted Deming's ideas.

Understanding the principles

In Figure 1.3 are the five principles on which TQM is founded. During the course of the book, we explore these concepts and show how you can apply them.

The five principles of TQM
1. Concentrate on the customer
● Be customer focused.

2. Do it right
● Do it right first time.

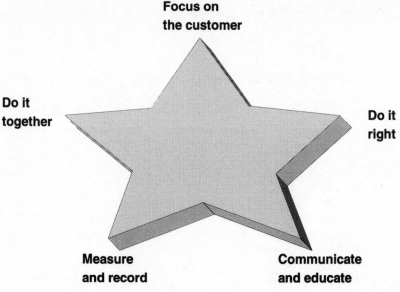

Figure 1.3 The five principles of TQM

- Constantly improve.
- Quality is an attitude, not an inspection process.

3. *Communicate and educate*
- Tell staff what is going on.
- Educate and train.

4. *Measure and record*
- Measure the work.

5. *Do it together*
- Top management must be involved.
- Empower the staff.
- Make the business a good place to work.
- Introduce teamworking.
- Organise by process, not by function.

12 TQM concepts

In discussions about quality, the above principles are bandied freely around. It is worth pausing for a moment to see what each of them really means.

- *Be customer focused* means placing the customer at the centre of everything you do. This can be quite a shock for the production-oriented organisation. It requires the company to check customers' attitudes regularly. It includes the idea of *internal* customers as well as external ones (a topic we look at in Chapter 3).

- *Do it right first time* means avoiding re-work. It means cutting the amount of defective work, whether on the shop floor or in the management offices.

- *Constantly improve.* 'Continuous improvement beats post-poned perfection', said a manager at Cummins, the engine maker. As the comment implies, continuous improvement allows the company gradually to get better. 'A 5 per cent improvement in 100 per cent of the areas is easier than a 100 per cent improvement in 5 per cent of the areas' is another axiom sometimes used by TQM people.

- *Quality is an attitude.* There are no shortcuts to quality. The old methods of inspecting for defects are not good enough any more. Everyone has to be committed to quality. That means changing the attitude of the entire workforce, and altering the way the company operates.

- *Telling staff what is going on* involves improved communication. Typically, this includes team briefings, one of the main elements of TQM.

- You have to *educate and train* your people, for an unskilled workforce makes mistakes. Giving more skills to workers means they can do a wider range of jobs, and do them better. It also means educating staff in the principles of TQM, which is a whole new style of working.

- *Measure the work.* Measurements allow the company to make decisions based on facts, not opinion. They help to maintain standards and keep processes within the agreed tolerances.
- *Top management must be involved.* If senior management is not involved, the programme will fail. It is as simple as that. If you are the big boss, there is no problem. If you aren't, your programme cannot start until you have the boss's commitment.

- *Empowering the staff* means getting employees to think for themselves. 'We pay people to improve the business, not just perform to the status quo,' said one organisation.

- *Make it a good place to work.* Many companies are full of fear. Staff are afraid of the sack, afraid of their boss, and afraid of making mistakes. In Spain, the UK and France, more than 60 per cent of full-time employees are very worried about losing their jobs, according to the Henley Centre. There is no point in running a TQM programme unless the company drives out fear.

- *Introduce teamworking.* Teamwork boosts employee morale. It reduces conflict and in-fighting. It solves problems by hitting them with a wider range of skills. It pushes authority and responsibility downwards and it provides better, more balanced solutions. Yet the culture in most companies actively discourages teamwork. So the TQM programme has to foster it actively.

- *Organise by process, not by function.* This element of TQM seeks to reduce the barriers that exist between different departments, and concentrates on getting the product to the customer.

Does TQM work?

TQM can produce spectacular results, as the following examples show.

- The reject rate at Bally Shoes fell from 2.7 to 0.3 per cent between 1990 and 1994. Lead time from receipt of order to delivery improved from 28 to 3 days. This followed training in team building, continuous improvement and waste reduction.

- Using TQM techniques, Courtaulds Fibres has gained annual fuel savings of £325,000, against management time worth £12,000 and a capital investment of £35,000. The payback was seven and a half weeks.

- Parcel carrier TNT Express has increased its customers from 62,000 to 105,000 in four years. Unit costs have fallen from £14 to £11 over five years; 91 per cent of the company's 6000 workers believes that it is committed to developing people.

- Rover Cars has increased its sales per employee from £68,000 to £126,000 in five years, a success which it attributes to its TQM programme; 92 per cent of its employees say they are proud to work for the company, compared with 69 per cent four years previously. Rover has launched 30 new cars in five years.

- TQM companies out-perform others. A survey by *Business Week* magazine showed that leading TQM companies (such as AT&T, Motorola and Federal Express) yielded a return of 89 per cent against the Standard and Poor's 500 index average of 33 per cent.

TQM is growing

In the UK, 25,000 companies have tackled their quality problems by becoming registered to ISO 9000 (BS 5750). Elsewhere in the world, registrations are also increasing, with big growth in North America, Brazil, India and the Pacific Rim. Many of these organisations are now seeking to build on their success, and are turning to TQM.

The first UK award for Quality attracted entries from major firms like TNT and Rover. In the USA, the Baldridge Award has been won by firms like Rank Xerox. If they take TQM seriously, maybe you should as well.

Is there a problem with TQM?

There is a major problem with TQM: 70 per cent of all attempts fail. A Gallup survey in the USA found that only 28 per cent of firms had achieved significant results from their quality initiatives (where 'significant' meant increasing profit or market share).

That is a gloomy statistic. But by reading this book, you're taking the first step to success.

Why it often fails

TQM fails because:

- Top management sees no reason for change.
- Top management is not concerned for its staff.
- Top management is not committed to the TQM programme.
- The company loses interest in the programme after six months.
- The workforce and the management do not agree on what needs to happen.
- Urgent problems intervene (such as a decline in sales).
- TQM is imposed on the workforce, which does not inwardly accept it.
- No performance measures or targets are set, so progress cannot be measured.
- Processes are not analysed, systems are weak, and procedures are not written down. 'TQM is an ill-described desire for performance improvement,' said one management consultant. That's a cynical view. But it contains a grain of truth. Too many companies try to adopt TQM without setting it upon firm foundations.

How does TQM work?

As Figure 1.4 shows, a TQM programme creates continuous improvement. This reduces waste and improves customer satisfaction. Both these factors ultimately lead to more profit.

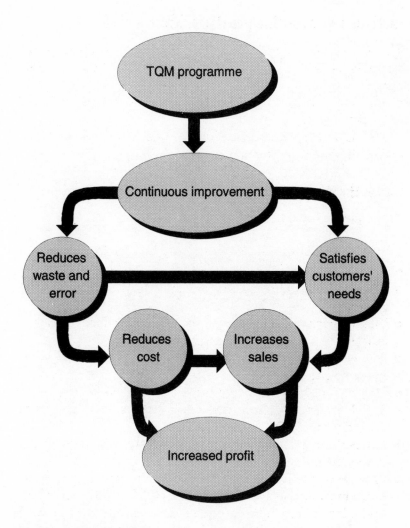

Figure 1.4 How TQM works

The benefits of a TQM programme

The main benefits of a TQM programme are shown in Figure 1.5. Some of these benefits are common to many 'quality' initiatives. Advantages which are unique to TQM are as follows:

- It makes the company a leader, not a follower.
- It fosters teamwork.
- It makes the company more sensitive to customers' needs.
- It makes the company adapt more readily to change.
- It lets staff from different departments meet each other.

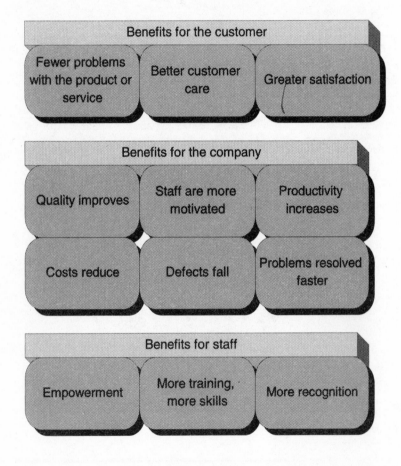

Figure 1.5 Benefits of a TQM programme

With this list of benefits, who could ignore TQM? In the following chapters we look at the main components of a TQM programme.

Self-assessment

This is the first of the self-assessment quizzes. There are others at the end of most chapters. This one helps you to assess the corporate culture at your place of work. Instead of guessing the answers, you can get the real ones by doing a survey of staff attitudes (see page 62).

You can use the quizzes as a benchmark. Do the quiz now and record the results. Then do the same quiz at six-monthly intervals. Remember that it can take five years to change a company.

	Yes	No	Don't know
Is your organisation aware of the changes taking place among competitors and customers?			
Is your company a friendly place to work?			
Are most employees secure about their jobs?			
Does the company widely circulate information about corporate progress and plans?			
Is your product and service as good as the best of your competitors?			
Do you have minimal waste and few errors?			
Are all employees customer focused?			
Is the organisation constantly improving?			
Score			

Score one point for every 'Yes' answer. Then see how well your organisation did.

6–8   A strong TQM culture is in place.

3–5   There are signs of a quality culture, but a lot of work remains to be done.

0–2   Go and find yourself another job.

CHAPTER 2

What You Need to Make TQM Work

In this chapter, you will find:

- What it takes to make TQM work
- The best structure for TQM
- The values and vision you need.

Decide why you are introducing TQM

You should know your goal. What do you need to change? Do you want to empower staff, reduce defects or improve customer loyalty?

If you know what you are seeking, you can organise the TQM programme to achieve your aim. Without a goal, your programme will lack direction.

Get corporate commitment

Next, you need corporate commitment. Look ahead 12 months. Is the company reasonably stable? Or do major problems lie in wait? If you can't commit yourself to giving TQM a lot of your energy, it isn't worth doing. If you go into TQM halfheartedly, it is bound to fail.

In particular, the chief executive has to be committed, and he has to motivate his board. Each member of top management should take responsibility for individual TQM projects whose success is crucial to the TQM programme. That will demonstrate their involvement to the workforce.

Devote time to the project

'We should have considered the time factor more closely,' said the coordinator of one successful programme. 'We should have realised we were taking on something that was going to take up a lot of managers' time.'

When TQM programmes fail, it is often because the management failed to give it enough time. If managers are told to carry out a TQM project in their spare time, it is unlikely to be successful.

Give it several years to work

Not only will senior managers need to spend many hours a week on the programme, but they will have to wait several years to see any results. 'People get despondent when they don't see immediate results,' said one quality manager. 'Then they start to lose interest in TQM.'

'It's going to take five years to change attitudes here,' said the operations director of a pumps firm. 'We held meetings and roadshows; we told the staff what we were planning to do, and they said they understood. But afterwards we found that they hadn't understood. With the benefit of hindsight, we should have done even more to explain what we wanted.'

Case study: A slow start for one company
At one company, senior managers spent the first 12 months exploring what TQM meant. They reviewed how the company operated, and sought a common understanding of TQM and how to implement it.

As a result, other members of staff knew little about the programme for some time. But senior managers wanted to feel confident about the project before taking TQM further into the organisation.

You need money

If you develop your programme in-house, you will have to pay the salary of a full-time TQM coordinator. You may have to pay for training courses. In addition, there is the time of senior managers and other staff. Employees will be spending time in meetings or visiting other companies. You may also print certificates, pens or mugs as give-aways. If you decide to use a consultancy, you will have to pay its fees.

One medium-sized manufacturer reckoned that its in-house TQM programme cost £40,000 in the first 18 months (including one manager's salary). Using a consultancy might have cost an additional £100,000, though some companies use a consultancy only for the initial stages of its exercise, and that would be less expensive. So before you rush into a TQM programme, you should set aside a budget.

When you have committed the company to TQM, and accepted that it will take energy, time and money, you still need personal qualities to succeed. These are shown in Figure 2.1.

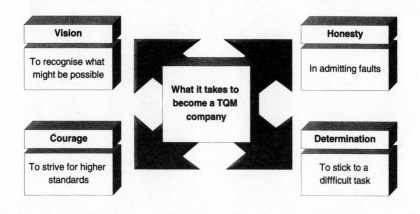

Figure 2.1 The personal qualities needed to succeed in TQM

Nominate a TQM facilitator

You will need a structure like the one shown in Figure 2.2. This has a number of elements, with the quality facilitator being one of the most important. This person will have day-to-day responsibility for TQM. He will not 'manage' it, because each individual must make his own contribution.

Above all, the departmental managers must create an atmosphere of total quality in their own areas. So the facilitator (sometimes known as the coordinator) will simply remind, advise and encourage staff about TQM. He will also guide the project teams discussed in Chapter 6.

The facilitator needs to have sufficient seniority to persuade others to adopt TQM. A formal job description should be written, outlining his authority.

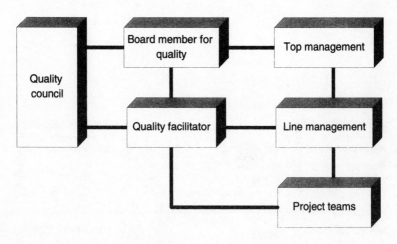

Figure 2.2 Structure for TQM

Nominate a director

In a small organisation the facilitator will report to the chief executive. In larger organisations, he might report to another member of the board.

Whoever has responsibility must be committed to the success of the project, and must be at the company's top level of management. Otherwise, the TQM programme will not receive the resources and authority it needs.

Case study: Making a quality council work
At one company which had enthusiastically embraced TQM, the quality council met monthly and comprised 17 people. This included all the directors and senior executives.

With so many people around the table, progress was slow. So the company decided to split up the committee. There would be a *core council* (consisting of four senior executives and two directors) which would meet monthly.

The core council would be joined every second month by the *full group*. This would allow all the senior managers to make recommendations and see what progress was being made, without delaying progress.

Set up a quality council

The quality council (sometimes called a steering committee) comprises a group of top managers and takes decisions on TQM matters.

- The council lets senior management discuss major TQM areas such as communication, internal customers and customers' needs.

- It also sets up project teams (which are discussed in Chapter 6).

- It evaluates the recommendations of these teams, and decides what action should be taken.

- The council also makes awards to employees who contribute to the quality programme.

The quality council should comprise the quality manager or TQM facilitator, senior line management (such as production and marketing), and at least one member of the board. The roles of line managers and the improvement teams are discussed in the chapters that follow.

See how other firms do it

If you want to see how TQM works, visit another non-competing company. The TQM manager will usually be pleased to show you around. Often a group of your employees can make a visit. The visits will help you to see the benefits of TQM, and you can learn how it should be applied.

Values, vision and mission

To succeed, the top management must start by agreeing their values, vision and mission.

- *Values*. What does the company hold dear? Is it shareholder profit? Are the directors planning to build the company so that they can float it on the stock market and become rich? Or do they want to build a strong company where every employee takes a share of the rewards?

- *The vision* is what the company could be like in five years' time. A vision will help you through the difficult parts of the TQM programme. Without a vision, people will ask: 'Why are we bothering with all this?'

- *The mission*. What market does the company want to be in? Do you want to be a world-class component business? Do you aim to have a health club in every major city? Unless staff know the company's goal, everyone will pull in different directions.

Do you need a mission statement?
Too much emphasis on mission and values can lead to stagnation. 'Paralysis by analysis' is a term used to describe the firm that is so wrapped up in its own debates that it does not notice competitors overtaking it.

The problem with mission statements is that they tend to be woolly and generalised. Most of them say, 'We aim to be the best.' Every company wants to 'achieve sustained, profitable growth'. All businesses want to provide 'healthy and safe working conditions'.

These are admirable goals, but they will not impress the workforce. Actions speak louder than words. It is better that the chief executive gets away from his desk and starts solving quality problems. TQM requires both vision and decision.

Adopt an ethical approach

TQM is based on fairness. It requires the firm to satisfy its customers, and to be honest and open with its employees. That means the firm has to be ethical. Every firm, like every human, has moral failings. Before a TQM programme starts, the company should carry out an ethics audit, and draw up an ethics policy.

The ethics audit should cover relationships with the government, customers, suppliers, staff, and the environment. It might include tax evasion, bribes and cartels. It might also involve the treatment of women and minorities, and the company's attitude to hiring and firing. Policies on Third World sourcing, offensive advertising, and environmental management might need to be formulated.

Be prepared for resistance

When they hear about the TQM programme, staff will be apprehensive and sceptical. They may even be vocal in their disapproval. Many of them will have seen previous management initiatives which have been shortlived.

Many members of staff fear change, because it could lead to

redundancy. Others simply prefer to maintain the status quo, because they are familiar with it.

Handle people's new-found interest properly

If you raise people's expectations, you have to meet them. If staff put forward suggestions, and they are met with silence, they will conclude that nothing has changed.

So when people indicate that they want to help, give them assignments that will allow them to contribute.

If managers have a dismissive attitude towards the workforce, now is the time for them to change it.

Case study: The problems of creating change in a successful company

One successful company estimated that it would take 5–10 years for people's attitudes to change.

It had a good share of the market, a willing workforce and healthy profits. Staff turnover was low, and many employees had been with the company for 10–25 years.

So some staff found it difficult to understand the need for change. In particular, they could not understand the need to work differently, when they had been doing things correctly for so long.

'We aren't saying they're doing their job wrong,' said the TQM manager, 'merely that there could be another, simpler way. Sometimes people do a job in a certain way because that's how they've always done it. People don't always know whether the recipient of that work really wants it.'

Manage investment

Staff will soon start producing solutions to the many problems found in the business. Some of those solutions will require cash. People will grow quickly disillusioned if their requests for investment are not met.

At one company, the telesales department asked for software which would let them track the contacts they made. The company failed to provide the software, even though it would have made the telesales people more productive. The telesales staff decided that the company did not value their work highly enough to invest in a set of PCs. As a result they became demotivated.

Case study: The TQM project that failed

A manufacturing company sought to introduce TQM. It called the initiative CWIP (company-wide improvement programme), and put a manager in charge part time.

The company also set up a steering group to examine particular areas of work, but no members of senior management sat on it. The group members each served six months on a full-time basis. Line management 'volunteered' members of staff they could do without for half a year. As a result, the group had poor-calibre members.

Potential team leaders were given a lot of training, but the training was never used and most people never actually led a team.

After a while the CWIP initiative folded. Many members of the steering group went back to new posts. Management realised that it could do without them, or wanted the opportunity to relocate them.

The lessons from this failure are:
1. Ensure that senior management is fully involved.
2. The steering group should be a line management review body that only meets periodically.
3. Let team members volunteer themselves.
4. Make sure that the TQM project is managed by a full-time coordinator.
5. Make training relevant to people's jobs.
6. Instigate other changes (for example, carry out employee attitude surveys).

The organisation should set a budget for capital investment; and should quickly assess the payback for each proposal. If the money cannot be found, the staff should be asked to produce alternative ideas which require less money. Low-cost solutions should be encouraged because they can be implemented more quickly, and show results faster.

Self-assessment

This self-assessment quiz checks whether conditions are right for a TQM programme.

	Yes	No	Don't know
Is top management committed to the TQM initiative?			
Has a steering group met in the last four weeks?			
Has a quality coordinator been appointed?			
Has a board member for quality been nominated?			
Will senior managers participate in quality meetings?			
Does top management have the vision to see what might be possible?			
Does the company admit its faults honestly?			
In the recent past, has the company demonstrated the determination to see a difficult task to completion?			

	Yes	No	Don't know
Does the company seek higher standards than those accepted by ordinary businesses?			
Does the company behave ethically towards customers, competitors and suppliers?			
Score			

Score one point for every 'Yes' answer. Then see how well you did.

7–10   The company demonstrates a strong commitment towards TQM.

4–6   Before you can implement a TQM programme, you will have to change attitudes at the top.

0–3   There is no point in trying to set up a TQM programme here. No one is interested.

CHAPTER 3

How to Improve Customer Satisfaction

In this chapter we examine:

- How to find out what your customers want
- How to get closer to your customers
- How to improve service
- The needs of internal customers.

Customers are the people who buy your product – right? Well, that's partly right. In TQM, there are two types of customer. There are *external* customers, the most important people in the universe. And there are *internal* customers, the people in your organisation who get a product or service from someone else in the firm. In this chapter, we look first at the external customers, and then the internal ones.

Keeping the customer satisfied

Today, most organisations have to work hard to keep their customers satisfied. To do that, they have to stop making mistakes in production and customer service. But eliminating errors is just the first stage.

Customers can be satisfied with your service, *and still buy from a competitor*. Maybe they want the excitement of change, or perhaps your competitor offers them more.

So you should *exceed* the customer's expectations, and make him delighted. This means giving the customer more than he ever thought possible. You need to stay ahead of your customer, by working out what he will want next year.

This is especially important in mature markets, where keeping a customer, and getting the most business from him, is a better strategy than finding new customers. It also means that manufacturers should treat retailers as business partners, not as a mere collection point for the consumer.

Do a customer survey

To achieve customer satisfaction, you have to understand your customers' needs. You do this by carrying out customer surveys. They tell you where you are failing, so that you can rectify any faults. Here are some typical topics:

- What factors are important to your customers? (Is it fashionable design, fast delivery, or after-sales support?)
- How do you perform on those measures?
- How well do your competitors perform?
- What do customers think of you? (Are you seen as friendly or arrogant, efficient or sloppy?)

These questions are very simple, but few companies ask them. Grocery manufacturers spend hours every month poring over the details of brand share movements. Yet the brand share is rather like the scoreboard at a football ground. It's more important to see what is happening out on the pitch. There, you can see what mistakes are being made, and what the competitors are doing.

You can use the market research data to measure your progress towards total quality. One financial institution has identified 25 factors vital to customer satisfaction. Every three months, it checks the reaction of a sample of customers on those 25 factors. In three years of TQM activity, satisfaction on these measures has risen 35 per cent, revealing a substantial improvement.

Other firms categorise their customers according to whether they are 'dissatisfied', 'quite satisfied' or 'very satisfied'. Then they aim to move each group into the next higher category.

Sometimes, conventional questionnaires are not flexible enough to let customers explore the subject properly. In such cases, *group discussions* allow small numbers of customers to talk about their purchasing behaviour in greater detail.

Companies who are involved with the public (such as hotels, restaurants and car hire firms) often leave forms where customers can write comments. This is, in theory, a good way to catch complaints. But not every dissatisfied customer fills them out, and not all companies act on the comments. *Mystery shoppers* can provide valuable information about staff and service quality.

Case study: How shoppers see staff
In a survey by Verdict Research, almost one in two shoppers felt that service in British shops had deteriorated over the past five years; 75 per cent said that poor service would stop them from returning to a retail outlet.

Shoppers said that staff were particularly unsatisfactory when it came to buying goods such as hi-fis and washing machines. They described the experience as confusing and intimidating. Almost a third of shoppers were suspicious of shops which appeared to have permanent price-reduction sales.

Meet the real customers

It is easy to talk solely to the purchasing officer, and overlook the users of your telephone equipment or security service. Yet the users are often in a position of great power. If the purchasing manager gets complaints from users, he will quickly seek another supplier who will make his life easier.

Some firms send their staff out to talk to customers face to face. This improves the level of customer contact, and provides managers with unfiltered customer feedback.

Get close to customers

The company which gets close to its customers stands a higher chance of success because it is closer to the market. There are many ways of doing this.

Communicate with them more often. Newsletters and direct mail keep customers in touch.

Spend more time with the customers. You cannot expect to keep getting orders from people you never meet.

Share information. You can reveal cost information to your major customer. Or you can talk about restoring vintage cars, if that is what interests him.

Target loyal customers. Loyalty building programmes can capture the 20 per cent of customers who provide 80 per cent of the business.

Microsoft, which has 90 per cent of the PC operating systems software market, says 'the future is in more profiling. As the database gets bigger, we cannot afford to mail everyone'. In the UK it has a magazine for 15,000 loyal and influential customers.

Make your customer's goals your own. In the long run, the more you can solve your customer's problems, the more business you will get.

Be ethical towards them. If you are seeking to get an advantage over your customer, the relationship will never be founded on trust.

Get more people in the company to understand your customers. All the company's departments need to know about the customer and how important he is. Employees should realise that they have an important effect on customer satisfaction, wherever they work in the company. Customers are not the exclusive property of the sales department, and staff should be encouraged to make contact with customers.

Agree performance improvement plans with them. Customers are impressed if you sit down with them and discuss your weaknesses.

Provide customers with additional products or services. This can involve training customers' staff, providing technical information or consultancy, or offering a complete business solution. Or it could mean providing a design service.

Integrate your business with theirs. Some suppliers build a factory next to their main customer's. Others provide a JIT (just-in-time) service.

Make it more convenient for them. Providing a simpler way to buy makes a customer less likely to seek another supplier.

Set up a careline
What happens if a customer buys your product and wants to talk about it? What if the customer wants to complain? Among branded products, there has been a big growth in carelines – telephone lines dedicated to receiving consumer comments.

A customer whose complaint is properly treated becomes a loyal advocate for the company. Carelines also help companies to pick up new product ideas from customers.

A survey showed that 83 per cent of US branded products carried a 'careline' telephone number. This compared with only 30 per cent in France, 15 per cent in Germany, and a mere 8 per cent in the UK.

Improve service quality

The steps to take in improving service quality are as follows:

1. **Get information**. Find out what kind of service the customer would like, and the ways in which the company is failing to deliver it.
2. **Have a vision**. Get staff to imagine what an excellent service might provide.
3. **Assess what you do**. Examine the company's processes. See where they can be improved.
4. **Create an action plan**. Set up a programme to create the excellence that customers would like. This may include staff training. It may also involve procedures for handling complaints.
5. **Set standards** to maintain your new performance.
6. **Monitor standards** to ensure that they don't slip.

Case study: How field service quality varies
When a computer, photocopier or piece of medical equipment breaks down, it can bring a company to a halt. So quality in field service is vital. Research by Coopers & Lybrand among 33 major equipment manufacturers (such as IBM, Hewlett-Packard and Canon) showed the results below.

Best %	Worst %	
0	11	Customer complaints as a percentage of total logged calls
100	8	Calls achieved within target or contractual response time
90	0	Percentage of calls cleared without requiring a field visit
5	50	Percentage of the field engineer's working day spent travelling

These results show that there are major disparities between the service provided by these firms. These differences are likely to be found in other industries as well.

There are ways of improving the effectiveness of field service. Some companies merely swap a new unit for a failed one

---

without trying to find out what has gone wrong. The service is much faster and the failed part can be tested and repaired back at base.

Few firms in the Coopers & Lybrand survey were above average in all measures. The best results came from companies which had goals, which set performance measures, and which had the vision to create major change. The poor performers did not know how well they were doing, and could not drive through the necessary changes.

Evaluate your internal customers

Every organisation has internal customers. These are the people who receive our paperwork, or who carry out the next stage of the production process.

We also have suppliers – people who pass work to us. They include subordinates, who may prepare proposals or budgets for us to approve. They also include upstream departments. Some examples are shown in Figure 3.1.

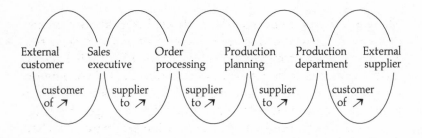

Figure 3.1 Internal suppliers and customers

This shows that the external or paying customer gives an order to the sales executive. He in turn supplies the information to order processing, who summarises the day's sales before passing the details to production planning. This department supplies a manufacturing plan to the production department, which in turn receives goods from an external supplier. Thus there is a series of supplier–customer relationships within the firm.

Problems facing internal customers

Internal customers suffer many problems. The sales executive may fill out order forms illegibly. This can delay the despatch of a customer's order, or lead to the customer getting the wrong goods. At the very least, it means that the internal customer has to spend time redoing the paperwork.

Or maybe the grinding department omits to send the paperwork with a product it has processed. The paint spraying department does not know what finish is needed for the product, so it is put into a holding bay until the paperwork is located.

Every day internal customers have to deal with these problems. It slows down the work and reduces productivity.

The training sessions (see Chapter 5) should ask delegates to analyse their internal suppliers and customers. Staff should be asked to identify the problems they get from their suppliers, and the problems they cause their customers.

The benefits of understanding about internal customers

Once staff recognise that they have internal customers, *their attitude to work* changes. They no longer turn their back on their product as it disappears on a forklift, or their paperwork as it disappears into the internal mail. Now they know that it is going to a customer, they make more effort to get it right.

They will also see that they are an integral part of a chain that stretches to the external customer. A flaw anywhere along that route will produce a dissatisfied customer.

Understanding about internal customers also leads to more dialogue about resolving problems, and a more positive approach to problem solving.

Support staff (such as maintenance staff, accounts staff and warehouse people) will also see that they are providing a service to customers. This helps them think how they could make their internal customers more satisfied.

At Girobank, the catering staff in the employees' restaurant now treat diners like customers. A changed layout and a new emphasis on the quality of food service has also led to increased use. As a result, the bank has recouped much of the money it spent refurbishing the restaurant.

Self-assessment

This quiz examines whether the company is customer focused.

	Yes	No	Don't know
Are the needs of customers paramount in your organisation?			
Apart from sales people, are many members of staff involved with customers?			
Does the company regularly and formally measure customers' needs and satisfaction?			
Does the company provide means for customers to make complaints and comments?			
Do you communicate frequently with customers?			
Are customer complaints handled quickly and positively?			
Is there a programme for improving your service?			
Does the organisation set out to increase customer loyalty?			
Are staff aware of internal customers?			

	Yes	No	Don't know
Does the company spend time improving its service to internal customers?			
Score			

Score one mark for every 'Yes' answer. Then see how well you fared.

7–10   Your company is strongly focused on the customer. This bodes well for the future.

4–6   The company's attitude towards its customers is about average. There is a long way to go to achieve excellence, but you can achieve it.

0–3   The company doesn't really care about its customers. A radical overhaul of attitudes is needed.

CHAPTER 4

Help Your Managers to Become Leaders

In this chapter, you'll learn:

- The right corporate structure
- Why you should organise staff by process, not function
- How to understand managers' behaviour
- How to start team briefings.

Which of the four structures in Figure 4.1 resembles your organisation? As we shall see, a TQM culture flourishes in only one of them.

In an **autocracy**, one person is at the centre of the business. Nothing happens without his approval. This is the management style of Stalin — and the very small business. In an autocracy, the only initiatives come from the centre. Everyone else obeys orders. This does not create TQM.

In the **feudal** company, people at the top are far away from the bottom, and the two never talk. The structure is rigid, so that the serfs can barely hope to become freemen, with no chance of becoming a noble, let alone the King. This system breeds apathy and resentment.

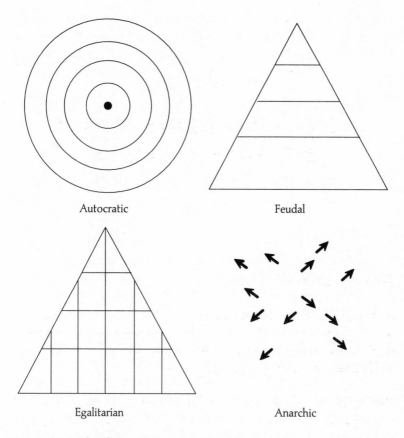

Autocratic	Feudal
Egalitarian	Anarchic

Figure 4.1 The four management structures

The **egalitarian** company is a much more liberated place to work. Here people communicate both up and down their own department and across to other departments. Teams can be formed to solve particular problems. Because the structure is flexible, it can grow and contract in response to the market. This is the TQM culture.

In the **anarchic** firm, each department makes its own rules. Every individual or business unit is isolated from the others, and the firm loses the benefits of a corporate approach. A management consultancy with 700 staff admits that it has 700 one-man bands. This structure is vulnerable. Top management has no power to stop a maverick from acting as he wishes, as Barings Bank found when Nick Leeson, one of its dealers, lost over £600 million on the Japanese stock market.

Getting the right structure depends on the calibre of the chief executive. But even small changes in corporate structure can help to liberate and empower the company's staff.

What does the company think of its staff?

After years of research, Deming and Juran, internationally respected quality gurus, concluded that staff are responsible for only 6 to 15 per cent of any company's failings.

In other words, poor systems and weak management cause 85 to 94 per cent of the problems.

That is an important finding. It means that all those slogans exhorting staff to 'do it right first time' are a waste of time. Most of the problems lie outside the control of the workforce. Criticising staff for being careless or workshy is misplaced.

Founded in 1783, Brintons Carpets believes that 'many quality problems arise because someone somewhere cannot do his or her job properly. It may be because of faulty equipment, inadequate systems or even lack of training'.

It also means that setting arbitrary targets (including zero defects) without giving staff the tools to achieve them, will only make staff feel frustrated and resentful. Those kinds of goal can only be achieved by distorting the system (for example, by artificially bringing forward sales or by 'cooking the books').

Case study: The dangers of arbitrary goals, and the company that didn't listen to its staff
One of the country's biggest construction firms had a small £14 million division which refurbished buildings. The divisional boss, a highly successful manager, was called into a meeting, and told that his target for the following year was £20 million.

'I can't meet that target,' he said. 'The number of enquiries and tenders is falling. In six months' time, we'll have fewer contracts. The industry is heading for a downturn. I think we'll achieve only £8 million next year.'

The chief executive did not listen. He told the manager to meet the target or lose his job. 'We don't need your kind of negative thinking,' he said.

The divisional boss went back to his business. He knew that he couldn't meet the target. He had a nervous breakdown, and resigned.

A year later, the recession arrived, as the executive had forecast, and bit deep into the construction industry. The division achieved a turnover of just £6 million.

So the successful TQM company recognises that staff can only achieve the best results when the culture is right and when the bad systems have been overhauled. It all starts with management.

Allocate management responsibilities

Consultants often tell disorganised firms (or ones which have grown rapidly) to set up *job descriptions* and *organisation charts*. That helps staff know what is expected of them. It eliminates the stress of having more than one boss, and ensures that someone takes responsibility for every important area. In smaller firms, this exercise sometimes reveals that no one is responsible for finance, marketing or the TQM programme.

Organise by process not function

In their efforts to break loose from the shackles of traditional departmental structure, some companies are restructuring along process lines. This means setting up cells of workers. In manufacturing, each cell may have its own dedicated maintenance and engineering staff. It may mean that a group

BEFORE

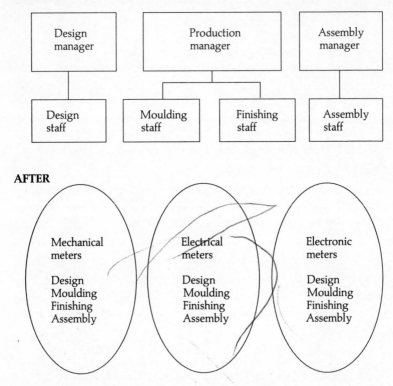

Figure 4.2 Converting to a process structure

becomes responsible for all the company's frozen food products, or all the company's personal pension products.

Figure 4.2 shows how a traditional structure could be converted into one based on processes.

Reduce management layers

At one time, there were many layers of management. Now companies boast that there are only three levels between the chairman and the cleaner. A flat structure has many advantages. People can't pass the buck to a higher authority, and they feel empowered. There are fewer people to say 'no', and the chances of a failure are outweighed by the new-found freedom to be productive.

But there is less opportunity to progress up the ladder. This can be overcome by giving people experience in more departments, and by encouraging sideways moves. TQM companies also encourage their staff to undertake projects, which provides training and job enrichment.

Identifying management attitudes

Today's manager is judged on his output and his ability to develop a team. As the managerial grid shows (Figure 4.3), some managers are better than others.

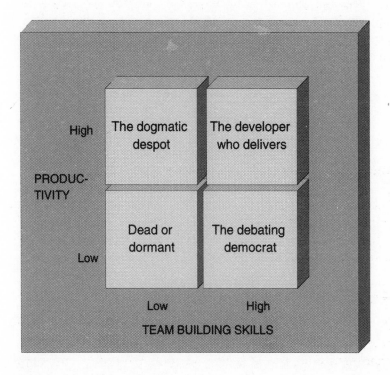

Figure 4.3 The managerial grid

The dogmatic despot gives orders and does not expect subordinates to question those orders. He does not listen to advice, and is prone to outbursts of temper. He shows no loyalty to subordinates.

Dead or dormant is not involved with subordinates. He makes few decisions, and the work carries on around him. His removal would make little difference to the organisation.

The debating democrat encourages subordinates to find solutions. He cares about his subordinates, and is loyal to them. But he shows few leadership skills and shirks difficult decisions.

The developer who delivers is aware of the company's goals and the needs of his staff. He tries to meet both these goals. He does this by building his subordinates' skills, and by helping them to be successful.

Training managers in TQM

Few managers are perfect. By getting them to complete an attitudinal questionnaire, the company can understand their views. It can then help them to alter their behaviour by training them in TQM skills.

These include team building, managing and developing subordinates. They also cover communication, listening, coaching and mentoring. Finally, they include time management, interviewing, technical and business skills.

Develop a core of workers

Some firms are outsourcing those processes which do not add value or which are not a central part of the company's product.

This allows the company to devote more care to its core workers, and to build up their loyalty and skills. It also allows the company to manage its peaks and troughs better.

Make a commitment to staff

When you speak of 'change management', the workforce hears 'job losses'. To maintain staff goodwill, many companies pledge not to cut jobs as a result of the TQM programme (though falling sales would be a different matter). This reduces the fear that change brings. It also allows staff to suggest improvements, knowing that they are not talking themselves out of a job.

However, TQM programmes often result in fewer staff being needed in the improved processes. At one company the staff for engine assembly fell from 17 to 14, and cylinder head sub-assembly fell from 4 to 2. So the company has to be alert to the possible need to redeploy staff.

Reduce the stress

During the 1980s and 1990s, companies have continuously reduced their staff through de-layering and downsizing. The ones who remain get easily over-burdened. This can lead to mental and physical stress, not to mention court cases.

Another problem is the company whose managers feel they have to work late and arrive early. Ryo Sato, founder of Jemco, Japan's biggest management consultancy, leaves promptly at 5pm every day, to discourage his staff from staying at the office.

As we saw in Chapter 1, some companies have a *fear culture*, in which people fear for their jobs. They fear their manager's scorn, and they are scared to take any initiative. This culture does not foster a TQM spirit. People must be allowed to question accepted norms. This can only come about when top managers change their style of work.

Say thank you

Companies like DuPont recognise the achievements and efforts of their staff. This can be done two ways: by regular encouragement of all staff, and by a formal awards scheme which honours outstanding employees.

TQM companies commonly reward members of TQM projects with a special badge and a certificate which recognises their commitment. When a project has been completed, and a report has been presented to the company's quality council, the team members each get a silver pin. Exceptional contributions are marked by a gold pin.

Other firms reward employees who give customers excellent service. The employees can be nominated by their superior or colleagues, or through customer comments. Barratt the housebuilder has a quarterly award in each of its regions. The regional award winners go forward to quarterly and annual awards made at national level.

Adopt common personnel policies

A TQM company has only one dining rom. This lets workers see the management face to face. The canteen has to be attractive enough to encourage management to eat there.

There should also be a common pay scheme, not a separate scheme for production workers. TQM companies do away with the notion of 'hourly paid' workers. (It should also avoid piece-rate pay schemes which encourage quantity at the expense of quality.) If there are incentives, they should apply to all staff.

Clothing can be common, too. If the shop-floor workers wear overalls, so should the production managers.

At the Canadian-owned Mitel plant in South Wales, all employees are paid fortnightly, and all benefits are common. The staff even have access to legal advice. This means they can sue the company if they choose to.

Other companies are giving shares to staff, because it boosts employee motivation. A survey by Rutgers University showed that a group of 256 US companies, where employees own at least 10 per cent of the equity, outperformed the stock market by 26 per cent over 11 quarters to September 1993.

Improve communications

Poor communication comes top of most employees' grouses. It has many causes. Managers are busy. They do not feel empowered to give out confidential information. And they know that once you tell staff about the company's plans they will want to express an opinion.

At a traditional plant, staff hear news, rumours and falsehoods on the grapevine. Sometimes, they learn news of redundancies or investment from the local newspaper.

So a TQM company tries to communicate properly with its staff. Communication is a two-way process. It means *informing* and *listening*. To be a good communicator, you have to:

- *Give staff information* – about the company, competitors and the market.
- *Listen actively to staff comments.* Provide formal and informal ways for communication to flow up and down the company. These ways include noticeboards, newsletters, and team briefings.
- *Encourage employees to participate in decisions.* The culture must change from one where staff merely do a job to one where they contribute to the company's future.
- *Organise cross-departmental activity.* That way, staff get to understand their colleagues' needs. It lets them create links that lead to improved output.
- *Get people to explore common problems* by discussions and meetings.

There is no point in handing out quality manuals and other weighty documents. No one ever reads them. Many people don't even read notices or staff memos. There is only one way to communicate, and that is face to face. This means setting up staff meetings. It is time consuming, but it's the only way that people will absorb information.

Sometimes, information needs to be put down on paper, especially to remind staff what has been said. Written communications should be friendly, not set in terse or bureaucratic language.

Improve appraisals

Staff fear annual appraisals, which usually demotivate them. At the same time, it is essential to discuss an employee's progress and goals with him.

TQM companies have adopted a range of solutions. Some firms have upward appraisals in which the subordinates discuss their superior's skills. Other firms turn the appraisal into a counselling and coaching session. A third group of companies have opted for much more regular reviews, which reduces the impact of each meeting.

Start team briefings

Every week on a Monday morning, the team members at Colt International gather round a white board to examine the previous week's results. They review any special problems, and examine the week's planned output. Everyone starts the week knowing what they need to achieve, and how the work is proceeding.

At team briefings, the information is cascaded downwards. Directors brief their managers, who brief the supervisors, who brief the staff in their department.

Briefings are important because they give the workforce the information they so badly want. A TQM company is different from ordinary firms because it keeps its staff informed.

Briefing meetings have to be *regular* (at least once a month). If they are not, the intervals will get greater, and some departments will stop using them altogether. The briefings must *include everyone*, no matter how low their position.

The meetings should be *brief* — no more than an hour, or managers will begin to resent the lost time.

Team briefings are for *small numbers of people*: 5–15 people is often thought the right size for a team. In larger groups, the briefing loses its intimacy and the feedback.

The briefing should consist of a *core brief* and *team-specific information*. The core message, which is devised by senior management, is information which everyone in the firm needs to know. The team-specific information relates to the group's activities. The briefing will consist of three kinds of information.

- **Policies and plans**. This is news about what the company aims to do. Or it could be things that the company wants to happen. It might include diversification, a no-smoking policy, or an advertising campaign.
- **People**. This might concern staff who have been appointed, promoted or who have left.
- **Performance and progress**. This might include the past month's sales, output or profit. It might be developments in a factory extension or an export success.

The information should be *clearly presented*, using simple charts. Team leaders should be encouraged to take responsibility for the information, rather than saying 'I've been told to say that ...'.

The briefing should be *two way*. The team should discuss any points which it wants management to know about. Staff should be encouraged to:

- Ask questions about the company, and have them answered.
- Indicate how their jobs, their team or their department could be improved.
- Suggest how the company, its products and services could become more effective.

Launch a TQM newsletter
A TQM newsletter tells staff about the progress of the campaign. It can tell them about TQM ideas, and it can highlight the successes achieved through TQM.

Photos of project teams, with the names of the members, give recognition to those who helped achieve the success. The improvements should be explained using simple graphs.

Self-assessment

	Yes	No	Don't know
Is there trust between managers and workforce?			
Does the company regularly tell all staff about corporate performance?			
Do managers regularly provide feedback to employees about their work?			
Does management listen to employees?			
Are pay and benefits common to all staff?			
Is there much leadership and direction?			
Does management encourage ideas and suggestions?			
Does the company recognise and solve problems?			
Do comprehensive team briefings regularly take place?			
Does the company publish a staff newsletter which contains TQM results?			
Score			

Score one point for every 'Yes' answer. Then see how well your organisation fared.

7–10   Your company is alert, questioning and proactive. It is fit for the challenges of the future.

4–6   Things are changing in your company, but not fast enough. Becoming a proper TQM company requires more effort than is being made at present.

0–3   Yours is an old-fashioned company where little has changed. It is unlikely that the existing management is prepared to adapt.

CHAPTER 5

Bring Out the Best in Your Staff

In this chapter, you'll learn:

- How to do a staff attitude survey
- How to motivate and empower staff
- What TQM training your employees need.

Most companies *believe* that they have good industrial relations. But few of them know exactly what their staff *really* think. Many would be surprised by the answers they would find in a staff survey.

The staff attitude survey is an essential piece of research. It tells you what staff think about the company, its managers and its communication. By repeating the survey every 12 months, you can see whether the atmosphere is improving or deteriorating. In the section that follows, we look more closely at what a staff survey involves.

Do a staff attitude survey

In a staff survey you can ask questions about the culture, communications, job, training, products and customers, and working with others. Below are some of the topics.

Culture
- Is it a good company to work for?
- To what extent are staff involved in running the business?
- Does management listen?

Communications
- Are staff told about the things they need to know?
- How do they hear about things – on the grapevine?
- Are communications getting better or worse?

The job
- Are people satisfied with their pay?
- Are they satisfied with the work conditions?
- Is the job challenging?
- Are there promotion prospects?

Training
- Have employees received the training they want?

Products and customers
- Do people know who the customers are?
- Do they know how the company is doing, compared with the competition?
- Do they understand the products?

Working with others
- How does the individual get on with his boss?
- What do staff think about management?
- To what extent does cooperation exist?

In his answers to a 'climate' study, one member of staff said that he was rarely consulted before changes were made in his department, that communication between sites was poor, that top management was not prepared to listen to employees, and that he had received inadequate training for his job.

This was no ordinary member of staff – he was a director of the company.

Case study: The findings of one employee survey

The progressive Redbridge Council asked its staff what they thought of the council. It got good scores for 'interesting work' (77 per cent), and 'serving the public' (71 per cent), but did less well on 'becoming more bureaucratic' (62 per cent), and having 'efficient working practices' (58 per cent).

Staff commented on a lack of training and development, and felt unsure about the company's aims. Overall, employee satisfaction was high.

Sometimes an impersonal questionnaire does not reveal true views. In these cases, it is better to get the information through informal face-to-face interviews.

Having surveyed your staff, you should communicate the results to the employees, and explain what action you will take. Having understood the needs of the workforce, you can start to remedy any problems revealed in the survey. As we have seen earlier in this book, you have to create a culture of partnership. In the following sections, we examine how you can do that, starting with empowerment.

Empower staff

Senior managers should refuse to make decisions about anything but the most strategic problems. Staff lower down the ladder should be encouraged to make decisions for themselves. This is the principle of empowerment.

The company should not monitor each member of staff's every move. Staff should be trusted to do their jobs. Many companies have done away with punch cards. Others now let staff set their own working hours.

In many plants, the workers can now stop the assembly line if they believe the product quality is below standard. This reflects the principle of 'quality over quantity'. It is better to stop production than continue to produce substandard goods.

Empowering staff means that they will make mistakes. But

the risks of staff errors are outweighed by the increase in creativity, productivity and customer service that results from empowerment. Moreover, staff learn from their mistakes, and if they can't make mistakes they will never learn anything.

What percentage of your staff are paid to think?
Where is the 'thought line' in your business? That is the line below which staff believe they are employed to work, not to think. Few firms can afford the luxury of employees who don't use their brain. Yet the culture of many firms actively discourages people from thinking. Moreover, staff below the thought line, usually production workers, probably have the greatest impact on the delivery of day-to-day quality, because it is they who produce the products and answer the telephones.

Counselling skills

The TQM company will help staff to develop people-based skills, and this includes counselling. Counsellors help staff to overcome problems at work (such as bullying, sexual harassment, redundancy, boss–subordinate–peer conflict), or at home (such as debt, loneliness or marital rift). Other problems affect both home and work (such as mental illness or depression, or alcohol abuse).

Staff can be trained to become counsellors. This gives them a valuable additional skill, and helps employees to be more sensitive to others' needs. People with counselling skills are adept at getting new ideas from staff, encouraging communication and building strong teams.

The training consists of information about people's problems, advice on how to help them, and role play exercises to provide practice in using their skills.

Change job titles

It may sound like rearranging the deck chairs on the *Titanic*. But changing job titles can serve to break with the past. It is also a useful tactic when the jobs themselves are being transformed. Foremen may become 'area facilitators', supervisors become 'cell facilitators', and engineers become 'production service operators'.

Provide better working conditions and facilities

First Direct, the telephone banking service, has provided a crèche for 70 children for the 1700 staff at its headquarters. As the case study below shows, the crèche is part of a wider commitment to staff.

Case study: Banking on success

First Direct bank sees itself as a gateway through which customers pass to access their money, obtain advice and control their finances. Conventional banks, staff are told, are a brick wall — resolute but restrictive; secure but unresponsive.

As a new institution, First Direct was able to start with a clean slate. Kevin Newman, the 36-year-old chief executive, sits among the telephone sales staff, and is fanatical about the company's single status operation. 'The challenge for UK industry', he says, 'is to tear down the boardrooms.'

His staff are trained to treat customers as equals, and the bank adopts the same approach with its own staff. The company recruits staff according to their behavioural skills rather than banking knowledge. Only 5 per cent have come from other banks. Staff who transferred in the early days from other banks were not used to dealing with problems themselves, or examining how they could do their own jobs better.

Carry out staff training

Training is essential to the success of TQM. Training helps staff to understand TQM, and aids the process of change. Training can also achieve substantial business improvements as these examples show:

- At Sadler Tankers, a bulk haulage company, customer complaints fell by 33 per cent after its drivers attended training sessions.

- Training helped BRS Truck Rental to reduce its staff turnover from 30 to 10 per cent.

- JSR Farms trained its arable workers in construction techniques. In the low season, the workers built new farm units, saving £50,000 on prices quoted by building contractors. This also solved the problem of seasonal labour fluctuations.

- After training all its 230 employees, Maydown Precision Engineering doubled its turnover from £2.4 to £5 million, and has now won a £20 million five-year contract to supply aerospace components.

Who do you train?

Next we look at the different kinds of people who need training, starting with senior management.

Senior management needs to be made aware of TQM. They need to know what it involves, what changes it will create, and how to make TQM work. You have to train managers to encourage participation, devolve responsibility and create new methods of work.

The TQM facilitator (who oversees the TQM programme) should be given extensive training in TQM techniques, creating motivation and empowerment.

At one company, all five managers and the quality manager attended a two-day TQM workshop. They learnt what TQM was, and how it should be implemented. After this, the company started to train the supervisors, the next level down. But bigger firms will have other, more junior managers to be trained, and we examine them next.

Line management should be shown how to become listeners and mentors. They will no longer be able simply to bark commands. They will also be taught how to look for problems to solve and how to set up improvement teams.

Team leaders are the next to be trained. These are the people who will run project teams. They are often middle managers or production supervisors. They should be shown how to run a team.

Team members are employees who join a project team. They should be shown how to participate in a group, and how to solve problems.

Who does the training?
A management consultancy often provides the initial TQM training. The first staff to be trained will, in turn, train other members of staff. As the programme develops, the training should cascade downwards, without input from consultants. Doing the presentations is often a new challenge for many members of staff.

What training is needed?
As we have seen, each kind of employee needs different kinds of training. But there are many common elements, and these are listed below. Everyone needs to know something about these subjects.

Corporate strategy
- The goals of the business.
- The nature of the market.
- The types of customer. What customers want.

Quality
- The role and importance of quality.
- How quality failures manifest themselves in the business.
- Common causes of quality failings.

Problem solving
- How to think logically and critically.
- Problem-solving techniques.

Technical skills
- *For production staff*: the ability to work on different processes (multi-skilling). Though not unique to TQM, multi-skilling is a prerequisite for developing a flexible, more motivated and more competent workforce.
- *For customer contact staff*: customer care. Questioning skills, listening skills, telephone techniques, handling difficult customers.

Personal, interpersonal and management skills
- Leadership (team building, how to motivate, how to delegate, performance appraisals).
- How to lead groups. How to be an effective facilitator. Better meetings.
- Time management, successful presentations, and negotiating skills.
- *For team members*: how to work in groups. Personality types. Conflict resolution.

Get the right style of training
Have you got a proper training room? One firm refurbished a set of rooms to create a dedicated TQM training centre. This helped to demonstrate its seriousness about the project. As people stepped into the smart new area, they stepped into a new world.

The layout of the training room is important. A schoolroom layout in which serried ranks of chairs face a high table will tell delegates that nothing has changed. Arranging chairs in a circle or boardroom style around a big table will convey more positive messages.

How much training is needed?

To educate staff about TQM, you will need to give all employees around two days' training. For firms with large numbers of production workers, this represents a big commitment, not only in the costs of the trainers but also the lost production time. One firm estimated it would take 10,000 man-hours over two years.

Analysis: What do you want from your staff?
Every company has different staff problems. These include:

- Inflexibility: an unwillingness to change
- Lack of skills: too many workers can operate only one process
- Lack of initiative: people don't bring their brain to work with them
- An 'us and them' attitude: the workforce may distrust management, and suspect its motives
- Lack of trained recruits.

After identifying any skill shortages or attitude problems, you can develop the right sort of training. But, remember that many of the problems cannot be solved unless management changes its ways too.

Other kinds of training

Managers need to become competent in a wide range of areas. The Rover car company has its own two-year part-time course at Warwick University. Through a mix of course and project work, managers are taught corporate management, finance, quality, statistics and information technology. Beyond this course, there are training programmes which lead to an MSc or even a PhD.

Other staff are not forgotten. Large numbers of the 33,000 workforce have participated in personal development and learning programmes; 70 per cent of staff have a personal development file, which allows them to map out their career progression plans. Every member of staff is entitled to a £100 subsidy towards any tutored course, even in ballroom dancing, because it encourages individuals to get used to the idea of learning.

In its corporate quality strategy document, Rover identifies 'learning' as an activity of fundamental importance. The total cost to Rover is £35 million in direct charges and time lost from productive work. The company believes that this investment is contributing to its renaissance.

Make your training work

Introduce a training plan. This will assess the training needs of each employee. It will record what skills are needed for each process, and which employees have those skills. Training records will show what training is planned for each employee, and what training has already been given. Training should be organised for all grades of employee; and all types of staff, including women and members of ethnic minorities, should be encouraged to succeed.

Make training relevant to people's jobs. Training often fails because it does not affect the delegates' jobs. Often the training is a jumble of jargon and catchphrases. Sometimes, it consists simply of team-building exercises with a TQM badge.

Create training materials. Once they have been trained in TQM, the facilitators will 'cascade' the information to other members of their department. To do this, they will need overhead slides, workbooks and a training manual.

Evaluate training through feedback. At the end of each training session, get delegates to complete a course questionnaire. The results will help you to improve the course, and identify areas of weakness. Remember to feed back the results of each survey to those who have been trained.

Mix the delegates. Each course should contain a mix of staff from different departments. This will encourage a wider range of answers, and allow staff to get to know each other. Sometimes you will need to train a particular department, in which case you will not be able to mix the delegates.

Get a senior manager to attend. Ensure that a director attends each of the training sessions, perhaps to meet the staff over lunch. The director should give a talk, which will emphasise his personal commitment to TQM. There should also be a question and answer session. The director should be as honest and open as possible.

Make it interesting. Staff can be put into syndicate groups, and briefed to solve problems or make recommendations. They can also play business games, to see what Total Quality means for other organisations. Then they can apply the lessons to their own work.

Help staff to develop their careers

Staff want to develop, so a career plan should be developed for each employee. Staff should be asked what their goals are, and be helped to achieve them.

Job vacancies should be posted, and priority should be given to internal candidates. Jobs should be rotated to give employees wider experience.

Set up a suggestion scheme

Suggestion schemes can produce impressive results. Staff at the Life and Pensions division of Legal & General submitted 5000 ideas in one year, which produced £15 million-worth of recurring savings.

All staff should be encouraged to suggest improvements, and all suggestions should be treated seriously. One worker at a Japanese assembly plant suggested that a knee-high switch be repositioned at waist height. Though a small change, it would improve health and safety, avoid the need for him to bend, and would help to speed the process. The firm made the change.

Hold open days

Open days let local people come and see the plant. If the company makes interesting products or is a large employer, many people will turn up, especially if you organise attractions for children. The workforce may see their plant in a different light, because it probably never occurs to them that people would actually want to go to the site without being paid.

Another option is to hold family days, where the workforce's spouses and children are invited. Instead of 'work' being a place where mummy or daddy disappears into, it becomes a topic of conversation at home. The workforce may find that its plant is a source of pride.

Self-assessment

This quiz assesses the extent to which the company cares for its staff and gets the best out of them.

	Yes	No	Don't know
Have staff attitudes been measured in the last 12 months?			
Has action been taken on the points which emerged?			
Are the lowest jobs enriched?			
Are most employees motivated?			
Are low-ranking staff empowered to take decisions?			

	Yes	No	Don't know
Are employees actively involved in business decisions?			
Do employees believe they have a long-term relationship with the company?			
Does the company guide its employees' careers?			
Does the company have a good health and safety record?			
Is there much staff training?			
Score			

Score one point for every 'Yes'.

7–10	Your organisation treats its employees like the valuable commodity they are. By doing so, it is harnessing their goodwill and imagination.
4–6	The business reflects the values of many ordinary companies. It has some way to go before it can call itself a TQM business.
0–3	The company cares little for its staff. The best employees will leave, and the rest will prevent the company from achieving its potential.

CHAPTER 6
Use Teamwork

In this chapter, you will learn:

- How to introduce teamworking
- The two kinds of teams in TQM
- How to set up successful projects.

'We have to match Indonesian quality, at Indonesian prices,' said a worried automotive works director. He had just discovered that an Indonesian firm could produce a £500 Rover wiring loom for £8. 'Either we pay our staff Indonesian wages (which is an impossibility), or else we achieve major increases in productivity,' he concluded.

So how do firms achieve that kind of major change? The first way is to maximise the effectiveness of employees. In this chapter we look at how employees can work cooperatively.

Introduce cell working

Your job is interesting and challenging. You have flexibility in what you do and how you do it. Not so the other people at work. Many of them have mind-numbingly boring jobs. A chimpanzee wouldn't stick at some of them for more than ten minutes.

So change the jobs. Make them more demanding. Give

people the whole job. Let them work in teams, producing the whole product from start to finish. Allow them to meet suppliers and customers (the real, marketplace ones).

Cell working, as these sorts of arrangements are known, helps staff gain more skills and become more flexible in their work. It makes staff more committed to quality and improves quality.

Gradually, the teams will take more of their own decisions about their process. They will need less and less supervision. Eventually they become *self-managed work teams*. By this stage they will be specifying the raw materials, tools and equipment they need, and managing their own budget.

But don't expect changes overnight. And don't give people challenges that they can't meet. In one firm, an unskilled warehouseman was given the additional job of telephone canvassing.

Prevent problems, don't solve them

Some companies have big inspection teams. Their job is to find the faults that production workers have made. This allows the workforce to ignore quality, because 'that's the responsibility of Inspection'. This system merely find faults that have already been made. It does not stop them from happening.

World-class companies are now doing away with inspectors, and are getting the workforce to do the inspection. The team members put their signatures to the product, declaring it to be free of defects. They know that there are no further checks between them and the customer. It has a sobering effect on the workforce.

Set up project teams

In the 1980s they were called 'quality circles'. Today they have all kinds of names, such as 'improvement teams' or 'corrective action groups'. British Airways calls them 'customer first teams'. Whatever their name, they are an intrinsic part of TQM.

There are two types of team, as Figure 6.1 shows. The first, which we will call 'quality groups', examine problems in their own department. The second, which we will call 'improvement teams', are appointed by management to examine multi-departmental problems.

These two kinds of team are different from the cells that we discussed earlier. Quality groups and improvement teams are project based, and solve specific problems, whereas work cells are simply a better way of producing products.

However, when employees become used to solving problems in special teams, they grow accustomed to group working and need less supervision.

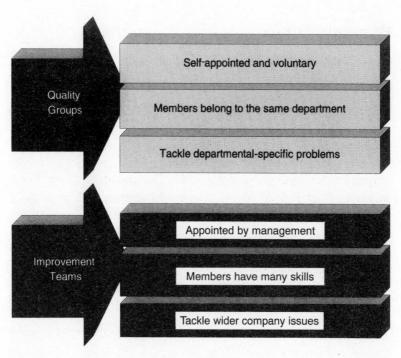

Quality Groups
Self-appointed and voluntary
Members belong to the same department
Tackle departmental-specific problems

Improvement Teams
Appointed by management
Members have many skills
Tackle wider company issues

Figure 6.1 The two types of project team

The advantages of project teams
At one financial institution, the number of teams rose from 28 in the first year to 1000 in the fourth year. By the fourth year, 300 out of a total of 1500 projects had been completed. The company achieved a 40 per cent reduction in inventory costs, an 80 per cent reduction in internal errors, and a 66 per cent reduction in customer complaints.

Project teams solve quality problems by applying the skills and latent creativity of ordinary workers. They also foster team spirit, and push responsibility for solving problems downwards. They empower staff, and give them new authority. They teach employees about statistics, finance, management and process control.

They also encourage staff to question accepted norms, to be dissatisfied with current standards of performance, and to look for continuous improvement.

Quality groups

Quality groups have the following characteristics.

Membership is voluntary
Staff may leave or apply to join a group at any time. They can also apply to set up a team at any time.

Groups choose their own projects
Normally, the group itself identifies the problem it wants to examine. Eventually, all members of the department should have experience of working in a group.

Groups adopt a problem-solving approach
Each group aims to solve a particular problem, or to investigate ways to improve a process. They are not talking shops. Group members need to be trained in problem-solving techniques.

Two things are excluded
Pay and conditions cannot usually be discussed, because they

need to be properly negotiated. Nor can individual people be the subject of a project, since personnel problems must be handled professionally. Everything else is suitable.

Management must be involved, and solutions adopted
Management must take the teams seriously. The teams must be allowed time to meet, and management must be involved in regular reviews. A director should be present at formal presentations. Management must be ready to adopt the teams' suggestions.

Group results are recognised
The group is not paid for the results it produces. But the company should recognise the work done by the group, in the form of badges and certificates, and mentions in the newsletter.

How to structure a group

Each group usually comprises members from the same area. This helps it to focus on a problem which is within their scope. Setting up a group is a good way to start a TQM programme. A group may invite specialists such as engineers to talk to it.

A group leader is appointed to guide the team to a successful conclusion. He is often a supervisor to whom the group would normally report. Group leaders need training in group dynamics and many other skills, as discussed in Chapter 5.

Improvement teams

Improvement teams are committees set up by management. Their members are appointed, and consist of people from different departments. This provides a wider mix of skills, so that a problem can be explored from all angles, and the solution will meet everyone's needs.

The team will tackle a particular company-wide problem which management wants solving.

What kinds of project should be undertaken?

Figure 6.2 contains examples of projects that groups and teams can tackle. They include technical issues, supplier problems, health and safety issues and process improvements.

Often groups tackle a long-standing problem. Occasionally, a new problem may occur, which the group aims to solve. On one occasion, the inspectors found that securing lugs on a motor were often mysteriously absent. Eventually, it was found that they were being knocked off as motors were lifted on to a workbench. The bench was lowered by a few inches to provide more clearance, and the lugs stopped vanishing.

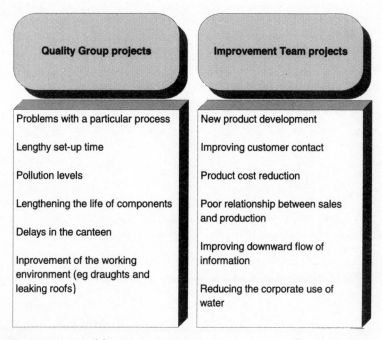

Figure 6.2 Possible projects

Setting the right projects
Projects should be of the right size. If the problem is too big, the project team will not be able to solve it and disillusion will

set in. One team looked at dirt on the surface of the company's products (tanks and drums), a problem which customers had complained about. In ten months, the percentage of products which were below specification fell from 67 to 1 per cent, while the percentage that was better than specification rose from 32 to 96 per cent.

Making the projects work

The company should set objectives for each project, appoint team members, and agree a date for the project to be disbanded.

The projects will take staff away from their normal work, and may include a one-hour weekly meeting in work hours. Teams should be given guidelines about this.

Information about the progress on each of the projects should be placed where everyone can read it. Keeping all staff informed about corporate progress is an essential part of TQM.

Case study: A supervisor's view

'I've noticed a significant change in attitude among people when they become involved in a team,' said one supervisor. 'They take a real interest in the problem and finding a solution. Currently we have 55 teams looking at problems throughout the works [which employs 1000 people]. Many of the projects have seen some outstanding results.

'People are more involved with their work now. Any time someone makes a mistake, they are berated by their fellow workers shouting "TQM, TQM." '

'However, you always get a few people who are totally against anything that the company is trying to achieve. They tend to be die-hard union supporters who remember the "good old days" of strikes and open hostility between managers and workers.

'Management is certainly better these days, being far more approachable and prepared to listen to what you have to say.

People are consulted more often now about changes that will affect them.

'It's primarily due to the deputy director. Unlike previous directors, he is very visible to the workforce. He will come on to the shop floor and talk with people. Managers now ask your opinion on various things. That rarely happened before.'

Self-assessment

This quiz checks the extent to which teamwork can be created.

	Yes	No	Don't know
Is the company production based on cells?			
Are there many quality groups?			
Are there many improvement teams?			
Do the teams produce noticeable results?			
Have most employees been members of a team?			
Score			

Score one point for every 'Yes'.

4–5	Your move to teamworking is advanced. It is bringing valuable results.
2–3	You have introduced many teamworking ideas. But you could go further.
0–1	Now is your chance to make a difference by implementing teamworking.

CHAPTER 7
How to Make Your Product World Class

In this chapter, you will find out:

- How to map your processes
- How to analyse and improve each process
- How to do business process re-engineering
- How to manage your suppliers.

Every activity (whether in manufacturing or the service sector) has just three stages. They are: the inputs, the process and the outputs.

Figure 7.1 shows a biscuit-making process. The inputs include raw materials, water and energy. The outputs include perfect biscuits and broken biscuits. The process itself is shown as a blank shape, because we don't want to look at the detail.

This is not the only activity that takes place at the biscuit factory. Staff also have to pack the biscuits, and send them by lorry to customers. There are also support activities like advertising and buying raw materials.

TQM improves the taste of the biscuits by improving the process. It also reduces costs by minimising the waste (the amount of broken or burnt biscuits). Because staff don't make mistakes, the company no longer has to buy extra flour and sugar. It all saves a lot of time and money.

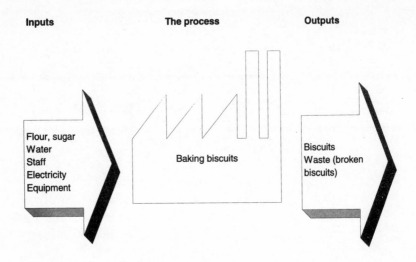

Inputs · The process · Outputs

Flour, sugar
Water
Staff
Electricity
Equipment

Baking biscuits

Biscuits
Waste (broken
biscuits)

Figure 7.1 The biscuit-making process

Map the process

Having worked out what its processes are, the biscuit factory can analyse (or 'map') them in more detail. There are two benefits from mapping the processes.

- **Mapping helps you to understand how the business works**. When produced as a diagram, a process may be revealed as tortuous. Often paperwork crosses the same person's desk unnecessarily several times. Sometimes the process works quite differently from the way it was originally intended.

  At one plant, a worker drew a process map which was so convoluted that the paper covered an entire table. After looking at the spaghetti-like lines, the team was able to suggest a simplified process.

- **Mapping helps to improve the process**. Maybe staff, when telephoned by customers, have to go to another office to check some figures. The staff could be given a computer terminal so that no delay would occur. DPC, a casting

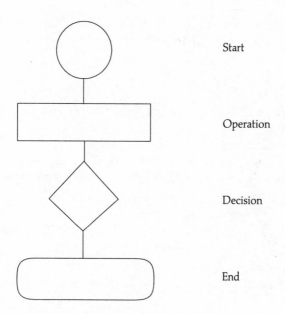

Start

Operation

Decision

End

Figure 7.2 Process mapping symbols

company, says that it has stopped 'component tourism' – letting partly made products travel around the plant to undergo different processes.

How do you map the process?

Standard pictograms are used to show what happens in a process. Four basic ones are shown in Figure 7.2. Using symbols gives a more professional approach, but many companies simply use lines and boxes.

You have to decide how much detail to show in your flow chart (or map). Excess detail will make the process difficult to understand. Too little detail, and you risk missing out problem areas.

It sometimes helps to draw separate, more detailed flow charts which show parts of a process. For example, you might have a box labelled 'test product for faults'. The details of this testing procedure could be shown on another chart.

You can draw the process using the lines and boxes shown

above. Or you can write down the process as a procedure
(which is discussed in Chapter 9).

Analyse the process

You should ask yourself the following questions.

Who is the customer?
Once we know who receives the process, we can ask the
customer whether he is satisfied. What changes might he want?

You can also ask, 'Who is the supplier?' Sometimes
seemingly unimportant people provide a crucial service, and
may know how to improve it. Hill Samuel Life Assurance
found that 53 per cent of all internal mail was badly addressed,
and cost four times as much to sort as correctly addressed mail.
It also increased the time it took to process work.

What are the inputs and outputs?
How reliable are the materials used in the process? How much
waste is produced, and how can this be reduced?

Does the process operate properly?
Log-jams may occur. Maybe the operators have to cut corners
or take risks to meet demand. Maybe the process fails at a
specific point. Can the process be simplified? Some companies
video the process, to help them see ways to improve it.

What happens when the process goes wrong?
A few processes have little or no impact on customers (in
which case they are probably unnecessary). But when most
processes fail they irritate the customer, or they hold up other
processes.

How is performance measured?
Many processes are never measured, especially in service
industries and in support roles. Being able to quantify how
much throughput is achieved per man-hour will give the
company more information on which to base decisions.

Is the process necessary or profitable?
Sometimes processes, such as PR, printing or computing, are better subcontracted to an outside supplier. Sometimes, processes no longer need to be carried out. For example fewer inspectors will be needed if the TQM programme reduces the number of faulty goods produced.

Who 'owns' the process?
If no one takes responsibility for it, the quality will drop. Improvements will never be made. It will be a Cinderella process, ignored and unloved. Allocating ownership to someone means that he will begin to take an interest in it, and start to think about it.

Case study: World class means not accepting second-best
A production manager who worked at Land Rover was irked by the noisy gear change. 'The gears of our Japanese competitors seem so much quieter,' he said.

The R&D people shook their heads. 'Our gearboxes are the toughest, and the finest in the world,' they said. The production manager was insistent, so the engineers stripped down a Japanese gearbox.

What a surprise they found. When they looked closely at the cogs, they found that the competitor had lightly chamfered each edge, so that the cogs fitted together more smoothly and quietly. This was attention to detail, Japanese style. Now Land Rover's gears are just as silent.

Improve your processes continuously

With each passing year, better products reach the market. Some improvements result from technology (such as faster microchips), others from better design, or from better process management.

All the time, your competitors are seeking to gain an advantage by making their products better. This is the theory of continuous improvement. If you don't seek to improve, you get left behind.

Small improvements are easier to make than giant ones, especially for people lower down the chain of command. Small improvements often produce surprisingly big advances.

Remember to improve not just production processes, but also management and clerical processes, too. The cost of manufacturing is often less than half the cost of getting a product to the consumer.

Case study: How to improve a school
Anfield School in Liverpool had poor results until a new head teacher arrived. He changed the school's name, got the pupils to design a bright new uniform, and put music in the foyer.

Then he set about changing the attitudes of teachers and children. The teachers thought their role was to contain the unruly children, while the children had negative views of their future.

As a result of changes, the school was singled out by the Schools' Inspectors for its improved results. One pupil said, 'Now we actually enjoy coming to school.'

This case history has a lesson for most organisations. For 'teachers and pupils', you could substitute the words 'managers and workers'.

Zero defects

Some gurus emphasise the importance of 'zero defects' (ZD). They point out that many firms make allowances in their budgets for quality failures. These allowances are an encouragement to fail. World-class companies do away with them.

You should expect to receive no complaints from customers. This goes beyond the idea of keeping complaints to a minimum. It indicates that the company should adopt a new approach, perhaps checking that each customer is satisfied with his purchase.

ZD is different from continuous improvement. ZD is suitable for a manufacturing plant where errors continually occur. Continuous improvement recognises that, even when no errors occur, there are opportunities to improve the design of the process or product.

Re-engineering

Business process re-engineering (BPR) is a recently devised tool. It is often used on its own, but it grew out of TQM thinking, and will help you to achieve your TQM goals.

If you are still doing things the same way as you did ten years ago, it may be time for a change. Sometimes you can do things faster or better by adopting a different method of work.

Take the selling of shares and commodities. In merchant banks, dealers buy and sell shares in 'the front room'. The dealer may then pass the information on a slip of paper to 'the back room', where the information is recorded on a separate computer.

This happens because the systems were designed decades ago. When the companies computerised, they designed separate front room and back room systems, not realising that the entire process should be integrated. In forward-thinking banks, the idea of the front and back room has been abolished. The dealer enters the transactions directly into his terminal. This sweeps away a whole layer of middle men.

To take a healthcare example, doctors used to want large hospitals where every service would be under one roof. Now they realise that these hospitals are very expensive. So doctors now try to keep patients out of hospital. Elderly people are encouraged to remain in their own homes. They are now treated at GPs' surgeries or in new, low-cost 'cottage' hospitals.

When undertaking a re-engineering exercise, you should ask yourself two questions:

1. Where do we fail the customer? (See Chapter 3.) Where do hold-ups occur?

2. How can we overcome those problems? How could we achieve a big advance in productivity?

Re-engineering benefits from techniques like brainstorming (see Chapter 8), which often produces creative, low cost solutions.

Until recently, inspectors at the UK's Inland Revenue would work out how much each taxpayer owed. Now the taxpayer himself makes the assessment and posts a cheque to the Inland Revenue. This re-engineered process has greatly reduced the department's work, so that 12,000 fewer tax staff are needed.

Develop a closer relationship with suppliers

A typical manufacturer spends 60 per cent of its turnover on buying goods and services. This means that suppliers can cause 60 per cent of the company's defects.

There is also a trend to outsourcing all kinds of activities, and this increases the impact that suppliers have on the business.

You have to manage your suppliers actively. One of the best known examples is Marks and Spencer, which has for many years stipulated designs for its suppliers, set quality standards, and carried out audits.

Your relationship with suppliers should provide benefits to both parties. 'Partnership sourcing' is a term used to describe a close working relationship with fewer suppliers. The corporate customer shares much more of its information with the supplier, and involves the supplier in the design process. The supplier becomes part of the company's team, and works with it to develop new and improved products.

This implies a long-term (even permanent) relationship between the two firms, rather than the work being put out to tender every year.

In many cases, the supplier's products are delivered straight to the production line. The company ceases to do incoming inspection of incoming goods, relying instead on the supplier's inspection. This reduces inventory, leads to Just In Time management, and reduces the cost of stock.

In turn, the company pays its supplier on time, which helps

the supplier's cashflow. The company also notifies the supplier of planned changes in production levels, so that the supplier can act accordingly.

There is a growing trend towards reducing the number of suppliers, with many large companies seeking a decline of 75 per cent. This allows the company to develop a closer relationship with its remaining suppliers.

Self-assessment

This quiz checks the extent to which TQM has taken root in your company's production processes (whether you produce fighter aircraft or handle planning applications).

	Yes	No	Don't know
Have you mapped and analysed your main processes?			
Do you aim for continuous improvement or zero defects?			
Do you have a suggestion scheme?			
Do you use today's technology?			
Do you vigorously control your main suppliers?			
Score			

Score one point for each 'Yes' answer.

4–5   You are a world-class company.

2–3   You have adapted some of today's management principles. But there is a lot of room for improvement.

0–1   Your production is rooted in the methods of the past. Things have to change.

CHAPTER 8
Improve Quality Through Simple Measurements

In this chapter, you will find out:

- What should be measured, and why
- Which techniques to use
- How to benchmark
- How to measure the cost of poor quality.

What should be measured?

People sometimes accuse TQM of being vague, and this vagueness creates problems for companies who want to achieve total quality. It is therefore important to take measurements. If you don't measure your initial performance, you cannot set targets. And without targets you have no way of judging progress. The most important measurements are shown in Figure 8.1.

TQM companies record measures which show what is actually happening in the business. These measures help companies predict changes in sales or turnover.

Productivity. Productivity is an easy measure, because all companies know how much they produce. The task is then to set goals for improvement. Accountancy practices measure

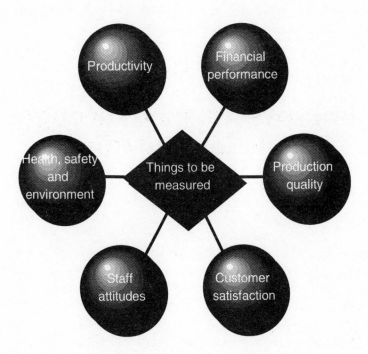

Figure 8.1 Measurements needed

turnover per member of staff. Some manufacturers have weekly marks out of 10 for various production issues.

Financial performance. Companies keep detailed financial records, but the figures are not always informative. This is why ratios are useful, because they track corporate progress. Financial information should be made more widely available: below director level, managers are often unaware of the company's month-to-month financial state. It is also worth noting that while financial data indicate success or failure, they do not explain *why* sales have risen or why customers have stopped buying.

Production quality. Much of this chapter is spent looking at ways of measuring production quality. These measurements apply to service companies, as well, though customer service measures may be even more relevant.

Customer satisfaction. The organisation should check how responsive it is to customers. This can mean speed of answering the telephone, speed of settling customer complaints, or delivery reliability. It may also mean measuring customer loyalty and the number of complaints. (For more on measuring customer service, see page 39.)

Staff attitudes. If employees are demotivated, product quality will decline, as will productivity. (For more on staff attitudes, see page 62.)

Health, safety and the environment. A power station will measure the number of accidents in a year, while a food processor measures the chemicals in its local river. Some water companies even measure convictions for pollution. In 1994, North West Water was fined 11 times. By contrast, companies in traditionally polluting industries are showing a downward trend. ICI was only fined once in 1994.

Taking measurements allows the company to evaluate improvements over time, and assess cash savings. It is particularly important to start records before an improvement project starts. Otherwise, the true effect of the TQM programme will not be seen. Once you have started making improvements, it is too late to estimate what the situation used to be like.

Taking measurements

Measuring the company's processes is often called statistical process control (SPC). Though it sounds technical, it is really very simple. To adopt SPC, you:

- Collect data for your main processes
- Analyse the numbers

- Make decisions based on what you find.

This can simply mean checking how many items are outside the specification, seeing where the problems are, and fixing them. SPC is 90 per cent problem solving and 10 per cent statistics.

At first, the workforce may complain about having to keep extra records. They may grumble that it slows them down. Only later will they see that keeping records and analysing the data gives them valuable information and more control over their work.

SPC is often used to predict problems. In other words, if the quantity of rejected items is growing, it reveals that a machine may need maintenance or re-setting.

There are many ways to measure a process and solve problems. Next we look at the following popular methods:

- Control charts
- Bar chart or histogram
- Pareto analysis
- Cause and effect analysis.

Control charts
The control chart is the most commonly used tool in SPC. It is produced by taking measurements at random, from as little as 5 per cent of the total production. Figure 8.2 shows that the process is gradually going 'out of control'. That is, the products are going beyond the limits marked by the dashed lines. This kind of chart shows trends, and helps staff to take corrective action before the product goes outside the specification and has to be scrapped.

Sometimes the data are shown as a graph on a computer screen. When the graph exceeds pre-set tolerances, the screen turns red and alerts the operator. At one British Steel plant, this has saved a £$^1/_3$ million a year on one process alone. At other companies, the computer changes the machine to bring the process back inside the tolerances.

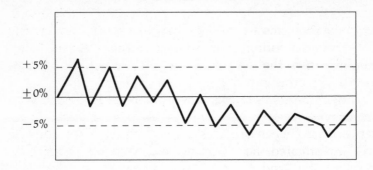

Figure 8.2 Control chart

Histograms

Figure 8.3 shows that the greatest number of faults are in processes 2 and 4. A different chart might show that faults take place on certain shifts, at certain times of the day, or on certain processes. This helps the company to track down and prevent problems from recurring.

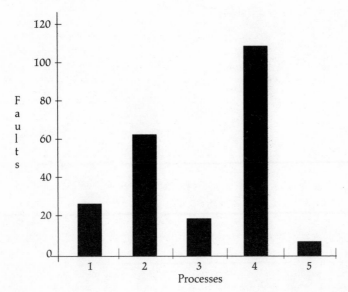

Figure 8.3 Histogram

Pareto analysis

A Pareto analysis is often referred to as the 80/20 rule: 80 per cent of the problems are caused by 20 per cent of the activities.

At a vinyl flooring manufacturer, most of the problems occurred when the material was put through a printing process. The other processes worked well.

The next stage was to find out where in the printing process most of the faults took place. The company found that the scrap occurred when patterns were changed. Then management investigated how to get the printing registration accurate faster, and how to get the colour balance right faster. This led to big reductions in scrap.

Cause and effect analysis

A cause and effect chart is also known as a fishbone chart, from its spiny appearance. It shows a problem and its possible causes. In Figure 8.4, a retailer is examining why sales have fallen.

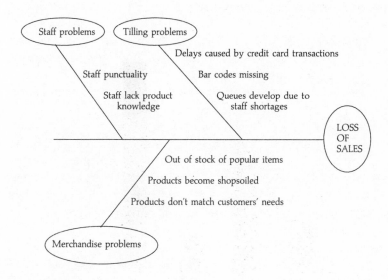

Figure 8.4 Cause and effect chart

Display the data

You should only use simple measurements. If people can't understand them, they won't use them. There is no need for complex statistics. The graphs should be displayed prominently, so that all staff can see progress. Some companies use large electronic scoreboards suspended from the ceiling. These can be quickly updated, and are highly visible, though they may not show the information as a graph.

Carry out benchmarking

Benchmarking asks: 'How well do we perform against our competitors, on the things that matter to our customers?' This might be good design, a high spin-speed, or technical support.

You find out (through research) what the important factors are. Then you investigate how you compare with your competitors. If necessary, you make improvements. In this way, benchmarking ensures that you are equal to, or better than, the best companies in the market. Figure 8.5 is a simple benchmark chart.

Three-quarters of the 500 largest British firms are involved in benchmarking. Mostly they examine the company's processes. How many man-days are needed to produce a turbine? How long is the set-up time for the injection machines? These factors affect cost.

Other processes affect customer satisfaction. BAA, which runs seven airports, monitors the length of queues at the security check, and measures customers' attitudes towards trolleys, loudspeakers and lavatories. BAA compares itself against Alton Towers and Wembley Stadium, which also have to park, move and feed thousands of people quickly.

How to make benchmarking work

It is not always easy to get the information about competitors' credit notes or service record. Measuring non-competitors' performance may not tell you very much.

Some information is published in annual reports, or industry

Comparative features of NTXM firms

Vendor	Product quality	Complaints	Price	Delivery	Network	Customer base	DB control
OUR FIRM	◗	◗	◖	◗	◖	◗	◑
GU Manuf	◖	◉	◗	◗	◒	◗	◖
Simpler plc	◗	◗	◉	◗	◖	◉	◉
Rockley Int	◖	◖	◗	◗	◖	◗	◗
Mead Electr	◖	◗	◗	◗	◉	◗	◗

◉ **Good**   ◗ **Satisfactory**   ◖ **Poor**

Figure 8.5 Sample benchmark

research. Other information can be gleaned by talking to customers. Some industries get their trade association or a consultancy to pool the data.

Some firms benchmark their performance against historical performance. But it is best to compare the firm against the best firms in the world.

Benchmarking is sometimes used by companies which fear they are falling behind. True market leaders tend not to look over their shoulder: they are too busy hurdling the next jump. So you would be unwise to treat it as your main weapon. Nevertheless, if you don't compare your performance with others, you cannot know how well you are doing.

Measure the cost of poor quality

There are costs attached to poor quality. Every time a production worker scratches a car bonnet, or you send out the wrong mortgage application form, the company has to spend time and money fixing the error.

The car bonnet may have to be scrapped. You have lost the

cost of the material and the staff time spent on it. Yet few companies know their true 'cost of quality'.

A cost of quality audit will reveal how much money you are wasting. Some firms do one of these before starting a TQM project. The cost of quality audit will reveal the scale of savings possible.

The costs include *internal failure* (you spot and fix the scratched bonnet before it is delivered to the customer), and *external failure* (the customer discovers the scratches; you recall the car, and have it resprayed). Some of the costs are hidden, such as the cost of lost revenue from the angry customer who never buys from you again.

One cost of quality audit produced the results shown in Table 8.1. Over 40 per cent of managers' time (two days a week) was spent on quality failure or appraisal. That was not much more than the time spent producing good quality products (in normal work).

Time spent on prevention is a good thing, because it stops errors from occurring, while appraisal is bad, because it looks for errors that have already happened.

Type of work	Example	%Time spent		
		Managers	Workforce	
Failure	Rectifying faults		18	**Bad**
Appraisal	Inspection	20	16	
Prevention	Internal audits	23	10	
Normal work	Producing goods	35	56	**Good**
Total		100	100	

Table 8.1 Results of a cost of quality audit

The company aimed to convert the time spent in failure and appraisal to normal work.

Case study: How Marshall Tufflex used the cost of quality to reduce costs

As part of its TQM programme, Marshall Tufflex, a plastics company which makes cable management systems and replacement windows, undertook two cost of quality analyses.

The first was time management for senior managers. It showed how much time (and therefore money) was lost in meetings and interruptions. Now the company has strategies for reducing the number of meetings and managing its executives' diaries better.

Marshall Tufflex also examined the cost of service calls in its window installation business. It found that most of the problems were caused in manufacturing processes and by poor communication when the order was taken. The company has now taken steps to improve both these areas.

Marshall Tufflex found it difficult to put a figure on the savings, though they were known to be large. The exercises were designed to help the company get used to the idea of cost of quality. But they have also made the company more effective.

Brainstorm solutions

Most of the techniques discussed so far have been statistical. But any organisation also needs creative thought and new ideas. One of the best techniques is brainstorming.

In a brainstorm session, everyone in the group is encouraged to put forward ideas. All the ideas are written on large sheets of paper which are stuck on the walls. No one is allowed to criticise any idea — that would reduce people's willingness to put forward suggestions. A target of 100 ideas should be set. After the target has been reached, the ideas can be sifted and the best ones used.

The session should encourage lateral thinking. One brainstorm session looked at the problem of hopper doors which, when opened, allowed coke to fall into a waiting lorry. The doors often failed to open and close properly, and this slowed down the coke deliveries. The solution was not to remedy the doors, but to do away with them completely. The company added a longer chute, and altered the conveyor belt so that it delivered an amount of coke which matched the lorry's capacity. This creative solution solved, at minimal cost, the problem of delayed lorries.

Self-assessment

This quiz helps you to assess the scale and effectiveness of the measurements taken at your place of work.

	Yes	No	Don't know
Do you regularly measure the quality of your products or service?			
Do production staff use SPC techniques?			
Do you display the information for all concerned to see?			
Have you benchmarked your business against others in the last 12 months?			
Have you measured the cost of quality in the last 12 months?			
Have you conducted brainstorming sessions in the last 12 months?			
Score			

Score one point for every 'Yes' answer.

4–6   The company is in control of its quality.

3–5   You make an effort to assess the quality of what you produce. But the programme is uneven and inconsistent.

0–2   Your organisation does not understand how to manage the quality of its products and services. Your production is likely to be haphazard and unpredictable.

CHAPTER 9
Adopt a Systematic Approach

In this chapter you will discover:

- Why ISO 9000 helps to make TQM work
- How to avoid common mistakes with ISO 9000
- How to assess your TQM programme, using the Quality Award.

Why ISO 9000 helps TQM

Most activities follow a pre-set format. Raw materials arrive, are processed, and then packaged. The same thing happens in a public library or a software company. People or forms arrive, information is processed, and decisions are made. Replies are issued, computer buttons are pushed, and documents are despatched.

But look at any of these processes, and you will see mistakes happening, even by dedicated staff. Production staff may use too much red dye or not enough yellow. An estate agent may send house hunters the wrong information. Records get misfiled, and time is lost searching for them.

ISO 9000 (also known as BS 5750 and EN 29000) solves these problems. In doing so, it gives TQM a solid base, with agreed systems that everyone can work to. ISO 9000 operates on the following principles.

Put in writing how tasks should be done
ISO 9000 gets you to write down how your main processes work. This means a new recruit will have information about how the job should be done. It also ensures that the job is done in the best possible way. Michael Page, the recruitment consultancy, found that ISO 9000 encouraged it to improve the structure of its job interviews.

Keep records
You should specify what records should be kept. If there is a faulty batch, the company can see what went wrong, and where. It can prevent the same mistakes from happening.

Do audits
You should regularly audit your system. This means checking that the written procedures are actually being followed. Internal auditors (usually from another department) will compare 'good practice' (as defined in the procedures) with what is actually happening.

Manage quality control
You should state where and when quality checks are to be made. This reduces the distance that a faulty batch will travel before being spotted.

Allocate responsibility
You should specify who is responsible for each major area. That way, every potential problem has an 'owner'.

Control the paperwork
If a bus company issues a new timetable, it is important that drivers receive copies without delay. It is also important to withdraw all the old ones, so that customers don't miss their bus. Similarly, you should manage your important documents, which include the written procedures. This reduces confusion, and makes sure that the company does it 'right first time'.

A new way of looking at ISO 9000

Looked at like this, ISO 9000 is just a common-sense kind of activity. It formalises systems that are already in use. You decide what is the best way to do things, and then you get everyone to adopt that method. This makes sure that everyone knows what their job is. It reduces staff uncertainty and process variation.

But despite all this, ISO 9000 is still a difficult system to work with.

Five reasons why companies dislike ISO 9000

Many companies dislike ISO 9000. There are five main criticisms, which we examine in more depth:

- It is bureaucratic
- It is internally focused
- It is imposed by a customer
- The company dislikes being assessed by an outsider
- The company doesn't want to pay for it.

Bureaucratic. Some quality managers construct paper mountains. They write procedures for the most obvious or irrelevant activities. They hand out huge quality manuals, which people never read. This can be avoided by designing a slimline system. ISO 9000 should be like a mountaineer's jacket: solid enough to protect you, but not so heavy that it wears you down.

Internally focused. Many firms lose sight of why they are implementing ISO 9000. They focus on their internal processes, not the customers' needs. A TQM company will set ISO 9000 within the context of satisfying customers' requirements.

It is imposed by a customer. At least one in every two systems has been installed because a major customer insisted. As a result, staff feel that the standard has been imposed on them. The company sets up a system just to get the badge. The ISO 9000 culture does not take root.

One manager said, 'ISO 9000 is just a piece of paper saying you have quality systems in place. TQM is about the way you work, about striving to improve, and thinking about what you're doing. ISO 9000 seems to be all procedures and audits. The only times you hear of ISO 9000 is when Lloyds come to do a QA audit.'

Some companies object to an outside certification body evaluating their quality. But an outsider will often spot weaknesses that are invisible to people who work in the business. So the certification body keeps the company on its toes. The assessors will point out the little slippages that the management may otherwise tolerate. Independent certification is a valuable way of maintaining quality.

Small companies don't like paying fees to consultants to set up the system, nor paying a certification body to assess it. For smaller companies, ISO 9000 adds cost. But those costs are usually recovered in greater efficiency. Some companies also get additional contracts once they can show they have ISO 9000.

Used correctly, ISO 9000 can help companies to perform much better. It is a lower form of life than TQM, but ISO 9000 provides a firm foundation for it, as we shall see later. Without ISO 9000, a TQM company often lacks a systematic approach to quality.

How to fit ISO 9000 inside TQM

In order to make ISO 9000 work inside a TQM business, you need to adopt the following principles.

Get staff to take ownership of procedures
Staff must map their own processes and write their own procedures. These must not be imposed on them. Avoid handing them a set of procedures which have been written by a consultant.

Make sure that all staff, including new recruits, understand the system

Everyone must be shown where his work is documented in the quality system. You should explain how the system helps him, and how it makes the company more effective. (If you can't do that, you have a faulty system.)

Give refresher courses to all employees. These courses should encourage staff to question the elements of the system. This will ensure that it remains a live and useful support.

Set standards to meet customer requirements

ISO 9000 can be inward looking. It is often implemented by production people, who want to make sure that it prevents mistakes. But sometimes they can overlook the importance of the customer. All procedures should be designed to maximise customer satisfaction. For example, customers may need to be able to talk directly to production managers, rather than pass information via customer liaison staff.

Have a bias to action

There should be a bias to action, not a bias to bureaucracy. If a tool breaks, the operator should go and get a new one, not write a request form to the maintenance department.

What the right system looks like

- In the perfect quality system, each employee knows how the system works because he was involved in writing or updating it.

- Everyone knows how their job works because they are familiar with the written procedures.

- The workforce uses the system to prevent and correct errors.

- Staff use the quality manual as a source of information, and to remind them how a product should be made.

So ISO 9000 need not be the enemy of TQM. It can be the reverse of the same coin. TQM looks at the corporate culture, and ISO 9000 looks at the corporate systems. Together they help the company become world class. (For more information on this, see my previous book, *BS 5750/ISO 9000 Made Easy*, also published by Kogan Page.)

Making quality programmes work together

As Figure 9.1 shows, several different initiatives can build a solid wall of quality for the company. Eventually, it will be difficult to see where one quality programme finishes and the next one starts.

Some companies start by introducing ISO 9000. That lays a firm foundation. They then use TQM to tackle people's attitudes. Then they solve particular problems by adopting specific tools, such as benchmarking.

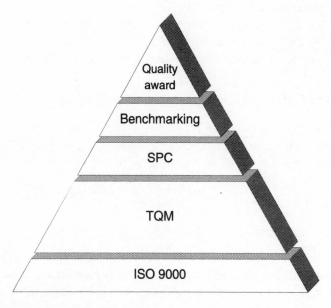

Figure 9.1 The wall of quality

But remember that there is no set way to achieve quality. You should use the tools that suit your organisation today.

The Baldridge, European and UK Quality Awards

Once you have started a TQM programme and attained ISO 9000, what do you do next? And in particular, how do you compare your TQM programme with others? The next step might be to assess your organisation against the UK or European Quality Award.

Based on the US Baldridge Award, the award uses the format shown in Figure 9.2, which represents the most complete TQM model available.

The award has several advantages. It uses a *self-assessment* format which allows companies to judge their own progress. It is also more *factually based* than other TQM models, and this makes it easier to quantify the success of your TQM programme. Companies that win the award can expect to gain favourable publicity and extra customers; all companies that use it should find that it improves their business.

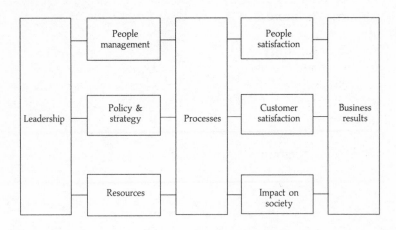

Figure 9.2 The UK/European model for TQM

Based on Europe-wide best practice, the model consists of what it terms 'enablers' and 'results'. The enablers consist of five elements (leadership, policy, and the management of people, resources and processes). These enablers are the methods which the company uses to achieve its *results* (the remaining four elements in Figure 9.2).

The model can be used to assess the progress of any organisation, including those in the public and voluntary sectors. The first assessment usually results in a full report, while subsequent assessments might be reduced to a checklist.

Companies normally start by deciding which site or division to assess. Then they create an *assessment team*, comprised mainly of line management who have been trained in the model. It can take two or three months to gather the data and write a report. During the assessment, the team interacts with the local management, and provides them with information and guidance. Below is what the assessors look for.

Leadership. This relates to the behaviour of all managers in driving the organisation towards total quality. Managers should recognise and reward the efforts of the people who work for them, and should be involved with customers and suppliers. (For more on leadership, see pages 48–56.)

Policy and strategy. This relates to the company's values and mission. Your company's policy should reflect a TQM approach, and your strategy should be properly communicated to staff. (For more on policy and strategy, see pages 27–36.)

People management. This element looks at your staff. You should release the full potential of employees. (For more on staff, see pages 62–73.)

Resources. How well do you manage money, information, materials and technology? You should be seeking continuous improvement in these areas. (For more on managing resources, see the sections above on ISO 9000.)

Processes. The company should identify its processes and control them. It should take measurements, and review the data. It should also be improving its processes. (For more on processes, see above on ISO 9000, and also pages 92–102 on measurement.)

Customer satisfaction. You should be gauging what customers think of the company's products and services. This will reveal whether you are satisfying customers' needs. (For more on customer satisfaction, see pages 38–46.)

People satisfaction. This refers to your staff. What do staff think of the organisation? Do they think the business cares for them? Can you provide quantitative evidence of this? (For more on improving staff motivation, see pages 62–66.)

Impact on society. Do you manage the environment? Do you reduce the impact of your operations on local residents? You need to be able to measure what the community thinks of your organisation. (For more on society, see page 33.)

Business results. This element considers how much profit or sales you have gained, as the just reward for all your TQM efforts. To score top marks, you need to show a strongly positive trend for at least five years.

More information about the model can be obtained from the author or from the British Quality Foundation, whose address is on page 123.

Self-assessment

This quiz assesses whether corporate systems are in place, and considers their effectiveness.

	Yes	No	Don't know
Is the company certified to ISO 9000?			
Are the company's main processes written down?			
Are internal quality audits undertaken?			
Is there an organisation chart?			
Has a manager been made responsible for quality?			
Do you investigate the causes of faulty products?			
Do you inspect products (or services) for defects?			
Do you keep records of audits or inspections?			
Have you carried out a Quality Award assessment?			
Score			

Score one point for every 'Yes' answer.

7–9   Your systems are well designed and properly implemented.

4–6   You have instituted a management system in a patchy kind of way. Now is the time to get serious about it. Do it wholeheartedly.

0–3   It's a wonder you still have any customers left. Get to grips with ISO 9000 now.

CHAPTER 10

How to Get Started in TQM

In this chapter, you will discover:

- How to introduce TQM, using easy-to-follow guidelines
- The right sequence for implementing TQM, and the important steps.

There are many TQM elements, so it can be difficult to know where to start. This chapter provides you with a step-by-step guide.

You will have already met most TQM ideas in the previous chapters of this book, and here they are brought together in sequence. Figure 10.1 shows the programme in a schematic form.

Action plan

Get top management's understanding and commitment

Decide whether you really need TQM and why. Don't go for TQM because it's fashionable, or because some consultant says it will solve all your problems. Work out what it could do for your business.

Unless top management really wants TQM, the programme will fail. You can judge the attitude of directors by whether they are willing to undergo TQM familiarisation training,

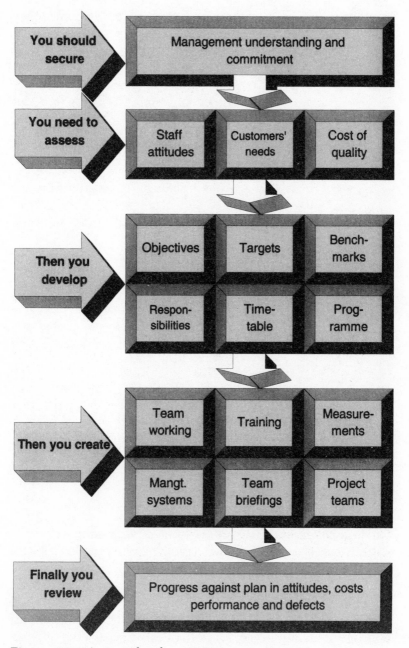

Figure 10.1 Action plan for a TQM programme

whether they will chair important projects, and whether they will introduce the training sessions to other members of staff.

Carry out a staff attitude survey

To be successful, TQM needs staff to change their attitudes. So you have to know what people think. By learning about staff attitudes, you can discover where you need to make changes.

Ideally, every member of staff should complete the survey. When you make changes, they will know that their voice has been heard. If asking everyone will be too costly, you can survey a sample of staff, and ask for a summary of departmental views from the whole plant. (For more on attitude surveys, see page 62.)

Assess customers' attitudes

You need to know what kind of service customers really want, and what problems you cause them. You can also discover how you compare with your competitors. This will allow you to target areas for improvement. (For more on assessing customers' needs, see page 39.)

Carry out a cost of quality audit

This is not essential. But many firms are surprised to discover *how much* money they are losing through errors and quality failings. An audit shows them how much they could save. It also shows them *where* the worst problems are, and so where they should focus their energy. (For more on the cost of quality, see page 99.)

Set objectives and targets

Targets serve to remind you of your goals, and the distance that remains. In its annual report, James Cropper, a paper company, admitted that 'little progress has been made against our ambitious target of a 50 per cent reduction in solid waste in two years'. It nevertheless won the Stock Exchange annual awards for published accounts because, among other things, the company had the courage to set itself high standards.

As part of your objectives, you may decide to write a vision or mission statement.

Set benchmarks
Work out how long it takes to make a product, or the percentage of returned goods. Measure the cost of credit notes, or other things that reflect your productivity and your quality failings.

As your TQM programme proceeds, you can then see whether it is having an effect.

Set responsibilities
You may work for a large or well-organised firm, in which case it will already have organisation charts showing who reports to whom. If you don't have them, now is the time to create them. Their purpose is to make sure that vital processes are 'owned' by someone, and that overlaps and conflicts are avoided.

Draw up a timetable
Nothing concentrates the mind like a deadline. So you should set up a timetable for quality circles to deliver solutions, and for surveys to be completed. Since you will be starting many projects, you will need an efficient system to control them. Simple project management software is now widely available.

Create a programme of work
You can't expect people suddenly to produce zero effects unless you have methods which help them to achieve that. Some of those methods are listed below. Set them in motion. Remember that TQM seeks continuous improvement. So you have continually to renew your action plan.

Set up teamworking
You can convert many of your activities into cell working. In some accounts departments, one person is responsible for loading invoices on to the computer, while another is responsible for printing cheques and getting them signed.

This makes it difficult to discover the stage that a payment has reached.

You can extend this activity by organising staff by processes rather than departments. In some organisations, this is called category management. For example, the Heinz Weight Watchers brands are now organised into frozen foods and canned foods, because that is the way that consumers and supermarkets buy.

Introduce training

By giving staff new skills, the company gains improved performance. TQM training allows staff to make fewer mistakes. It makes them better able to cope with irritable customers or technical problems.

Set up measurements

Measure the quality of your output. By analysing it, you can reduce the number of errors. Keep records of complaints, and measure customer satisfaction. These measures will give you a better understanding of your performance.

Introduce a quality management system

ISO 9000 is not as glamorous as TQM, but its mundane systems have saved many companies from making mistakes. Barings, Britain's oldest merchant bank, collapsed when one of its dealers lost £880 million by speculating on the Japanese stock market. For a year prior to the collapse, staff had pointed out the need for a system that would allow the company to know what was going on.

Set up team briefings

Team briefings are a strong visible sign of the TQM company. They show that the business is committed to improved communications. They ensure that everyone in the organisation knows what is going on. And they encourage an upward flow of information.

At this point in the programme, you should also be looking to improve communication in general. Team briefings are just one way of doing that. Newsletters are another.

Team briefings help to get *all staff* actively participating in the TQM project from its earliest days. If you don't, they will feel left out and threatened. They may become obstructive. At the very least, you will lose the value of their input.

As one consultant said, 'People don't mind change; but they dislike being changed.'

Set up project teams

Project teams allow employees to reduce the level of defects. They educate staff to understand how the business works, and encourages them to think about their work. They are a valuable way of motivating and encouraging the workforce.

You should explain what a project team involves, and then seek volunteers. The team leaders can be a valuable source of unsuspected talent.

Review progress, and continue improving

You need to monitor progress continually. You can do this by assessing the data which should now be flowing in greater quantity. You can compare the data with the original benchmarks. Have staff attitudes changed as you forecast? If not, what changes do you need to make?

You will also need to change the programme as the market alters, and as the company grows.

Decide whether to use consultants

Every firm is different. Some want consultants, while others shun them. If you decide to use a management consultancy, remember the following points:

- *The consultancy must have experience* in your industry or a related field. A specialist paint firm hired a consultant who had previously worked in the nuclear power industry. Because of his background, the consultant recommended grandiose solutions which were inappropriate for the client.

- *The consultancy should reflect the size of your business*. A one-man consultancy is fine for helping small firms. A large company needs the resources of a major consultancy.
- *Make sure you meet and like the consultant* with whom you would be working. Some consultants will not fit your corporate style.
- *Don't expect the consultancy to solve problems as if by magic*. Have a clear understanding of what the consultant can and cannot do.
- *Get quotes* from different consultants, setting out the work that they would do, and the costs.
- *If you appoint a consultancy*, agree a timetable, and set targets. Manage the consultancy. Set up progress meetings. Amend the project if necessary in the light of changing circumstances.
- *Don't let the consultancy do too much work*. Only let them train the trainers. In other words, get them to train your managers, who will train their own staff. Above all, don't let the consultancy simply compile a manual and hand it to staff. Use the consultancy to pass its knowledge to your employees.

CHAPTER 11
Further Information

What the words mean

BS 5750	A system for managing quality. The same as ISO 9000 and EN 29000.
Business process re-engineering	Changing a company activity so that it meets the customers' needs better.
Continuous improvement	The principle of continually seeking an improved performance.
Empowerment	Giving staff the power to make decisions.
EN 29000	A system for managing quality. The same as BS 5750 and ISO 9000.
Facilitator	The manager who runs the TQM programme or the quality groups.
Improvement team	A group of employees which tackles a particular problem of quality. Usually appointed by management and with a range of skills.
ISO 9000	A system for managing quality. The same as BS 5750 and EN 29000.
Procedure	A description of how to carry out a process. The procedure is written down

	and updated when necessary.
Process	Activities in the business, ranging from buying to warehousing. Often refers to production activities.
Quality circle, quality group	A voluntary group, usually with staff from the same department, which seeks to solve a quality problem or recommend improvements.
Quality council	A regular meeting of senior managers to review the progress of the TQM programme.
Statistical process control (SPC)	Simple statistics which check whether a process is conforming to specification.
Team briefings	Telling members of a team what is happening in their group and the company.
Team leader	An employee who manages, on a part-time basis, a quality circle or similar group.
Total Quality Management (TQM)	Achieving customer satisfaction by getting it right first time, through continuous improvement, and by motivating employees.
Zero defects (ZD)	The goal of total quality: a complete lack of defects.

Addresses

The Business Institute
Honeycombe House, Bagley, Wedmore BS28 4TD.
Tel: (01934) 713563; Fax (01934) 713492
Provides TQM consultancy and training through the PITCh programme (Performance Improvement Through Change).

Department of Trade and Industry
DTI Publications, Admail 528, London SW1W 8YT.
Tel: 0171 510 0144

The DTI publishes free booklets on TQM and related subjects.

The Institute of Quality Assurance (IQA)
61 Southwark Street, London SE1 1SB. Tel: 0171 401 7227
The IQA is for people involved in quality assurance. It organises training and conferences.

British Quality Foundation
120 Wilton Road, London SW1V 1JZ. Tel: 0171 931 0607
Promotes total quality management, and in particular the self-assessment model known as the UK and European Award.

National Society for Quality through Teamwork (NSQT)
2 Castle Street, Salisbury, Wiltshire SP1 1BB.
Tel: (01722) 326667
The society fosters team working. It provides training, as well as meetings and conferences. In other European countries, similar organisations are linked by:

The European Federation of Quality Circle Associations
(EFQCA), 44 Rue Washington, Brussels 1050, Belgium

British Standards Institution (BSI)
Enquiry Section, BSI, Linford Wood, Milton Keynes
MK14 6LE. Tel: (01908) 221166
The BSI sets the UK's standards, one of which is BS EN ISO 9000 (formerly BS 5750), the standard for quality systems. The BSI has a separate commercial body called BSI QA.